MATTHEW HENRY ON PRAYER

31 BIBLICAL INSIGHTS FOR LEARNING HOW TO PRAY.

GODLIPRESS TEAM

© **Copyright 2023 by GodliPress. All rights reserved.**

This book is copyright protected. You cannot amend, distribute, sell, use, quote or paraphrase any part, or the content within this book, without the consent of the author or publisher, except in the case of brief quotations embodied in critical articles or reviews.

Scripture quotations are from The ESV® Bible (The Holy Bible, English Standard Version®), copyright © 2001 by Crossway, a publishing ministry of Good News Publishers. Used by permission. All rights reserved

CONTENTS

Introduction	vii
1. ASKING A FATHER	1
Why We Ask Him	2
Why He Gives	3
Daily Reflection	4
2. THE HOLY SPIRIT HELPS US	6
Daily Reflection	9
3. JESUS' PRAYER IN GETHSEMANE	11
Daily Reflection	14
4. PRAYING IN SECRET	15
Not Like the Hypocrites	15
Praying by Yourself	17
Daily Reflection	19
5. SHORT, SIMPLE PRAYERS	20
No Useless Repetitions	21
Choose Your Words Carefully	22
Daily Reflection	23
6. ASK, SEEK, AND KNOCK	25
The Command	25
The Promise	27
Daily Reflection	28
7. WHAT IS PRAYER?	29
Daily Reflection	31
8. PSALM 17	33
Daily Reflection	35
9. PRAYING FOR PROTECTION FROM OTHERS	37
Daily Reflection	40

10. THE LORD'S PRAYER (PREFACE)	41
Daily Reflection	44
11. THE LORD'S PRAYER (FIRST PETITIONS)	45
Daily Reflection	48
12. THE LORD'S PRAYER (SECOND PETITIONS)	50
Daily Reflection	53
13. THE LORD'S PRAYER (CONCLUSION)	55
Daily Reflection	58
14. A METHOD FOR PRAYER	60
Daily Reflection	63
15. BRING EVERYTHING TO GOD IN PRAYER	64
Daily Reflection	67
16. THE PRAYER OF A RIGHTEOUS PERSON	69
Daily Reflection	71
17. PRAYING FOR OTHERS	73
Praying for the Sick	73
Confessing to Others	75
Daily Reflection	76
18. A PRAYER OF REPENTANCE	77
Daily Reflection	80
19. PRAYER IS ARMOR	81
Daily Reflection	83
20. THE ORDER OF PRAYER	85
Adoration	85
Confession	86
Petitions and Requests	86
Thanksgivings for Mercy	87
Intercede for Others	88
Intercede for Specifics	88
Conclusion	89
Daily Reflection	89

21. PERSISTENT WIDOW	91
Assurances We Have of Being Heard	93
Daily Reflection	95
22. USING ARGUMENTS IN PRAYER	96
Daily Reflection	99
23. THE PHARISEE'S PRAYER	101
His Arrogance	101
His Pride	103
Daily Reflection	104
24. THE TAX COLLECTOR'S PRAYER	105
His Attitude	105
His Words	107
Daily Reflection	108
25. DAVID'S PRAYER	110
A Prayer to Be Heard	110
A Prayer to Be Kept	111
Daily Reflection	113
26. SOLOMON'S PRAYER	114
Daily Reflection	117
27. PAUL'S THANKSGIVING PRAYER	118
Daily Reflection	121
28. NEHEMIAH'S PRAYER	123
Daily Reflection	126
29. HANNAH'S THANKSGIVING	127
Daily Reflection	130
30. JESUS PRAYS FOR THE DISCIPLES TO BE KEPT	132
Daily Reflection	135
31. JESUS PRAYS FOR UNITY	136
Daily Reflection	139
About Matthew Henry	141
Bibliography	145

INTRODUCTION

"The Bible is a letter God has sent to us; prayer is a letter we send to him."

Why do we need to go back to classic Christian writers when we have so many good authors today? The bookshops are full of intuitive guides on how to live as a Christian—every topic is covered, from money, relationships, and ministry to God, spiritual warfare, and heaven. Take your pick, they are all there. So why read a book written by someone who lived in the 1700s?

There is something that sets the writers of old apart from these modern ones. They have stood the test of time. Their works have been reproduced so many times because they do not just carry a "new" angle—they are steeped in sound doctrine!

Matthew Henry is one of those writers. We may think he is out of date because his books are over 200 years old, but the truth they carry is still as relevant today as it was back then. The same God we serve today, who directed the apostles and others to scribe the Bible, is clearly evident in the words Henry wrote. An undeniable truth that can only be inspired by the Holy Spirit!

Henry's most well known for his extensive commentary on the Bible. Delving deep into each verse, he brought meaning to the scriptures and knowledge to many Christians who had struggled to understand much of God's word. For hundreds of years, this guide has been the go-to when studying the Bible.

Instead of providing a technical methodology, Henry brought a practical and devotional approach for everyday believers. His heart was in bringing Christians closer to God through their understanding of the verses. For him, growing in a spiritual relationship went hand-in-hand with the Bible. Like many of his fellow Puritan preachers, the Word of God and the Spirit of God were vital for becoming mature Christians.

It was the reason he also published his book, *A Method for Prayer*. Rather than another book explaining the reasons for and benefits of praying, he simply laid out a technique of using the scriptures as a foundation to pray from. What better way to speak to God but through the language of the Bible? Drawing from many different verses, Henry pieces together prayers you and I can say, all of it biblically based. Both his commentary and *A Method for Prayer* highlight

Henry's perspective on the importance of the Bible and prayer. One cannot go without the other!

In this new devotional, our view is the same. That is why we have taken Henry's best insights on prayer from both of these books and presented them in a 31-day format. Set out to be studied over one month, each day offers a treasure of rich explanations of passages of prayer from the Bible from the Old and the New Testaments. A look at Moses, Hannah, Solomon, David, Jesus, and Paul gives us a unique overview of people who prayed in different circumstances, for various reasons, and in unique ways.

Each daily excerpt is like a mini Bible study revealing the idea, method, and heart of prayer. The only change we have made is to update some of the old language Henry used to make it accessible to readers today. Along with this, we've included daily reflections to assist in deeper thought. These are not meant to add to Henry's insights or to detract from them, but simply to guide you to think further about what you have read and apply it to your own life. Rather than throwing out the old and embracing every new wind of doctrine, we want to bring you biblical understanding based on solid discernment. Matthew Henry is about as solid as they come!

Our hope in bringing you this book is that you will grow in Christ, and grow in the way you speak to Him. Your relationship with Jesus is the most important aspect of Christianity, and if you do not know how to converse and communicate with God, then there is little chance you will mature. We want you to experience the fullness that comes with confident, humble prayer. We know that Matthew Henry's words will guide you to a fuller life in prayer!

"You may as soon find a living man who does not breathe, as a living Christian who does not pray."

1

ASKING A FATHER

*Which one of you, if his son asks him for bread, will give him a stone?
Or if he asks for a fish, will give him a serpent?
If you then, who are evil, know how to give good gifts to your children,
how much more will your Father who is in heaven
give good things to those who ask him!*
Matthew 7:9-11

The example of our earthly parents, and their natural tendency to give their children what they ask, is given here. Jesus asks those listening, *"Which one of you,* [even if you have a bad temper] *if his son asks him for bread, will give him a stone?"* He then reasons that *"If you then, who are evil, know how to give good gifts to your children, how much more will your Father who is in heaven give good things to those who ask him!"*

Why We Ask Him

To direct our prayers and expectations.

We must come to God as children come to a Father in heaven, with reverence and confidence. A child that is in trouble or needs something naturally runs to the father with its complaints. So, our new Christian nature should send us to God to find provision and support.

We must come to him for good things because he gives to those that ask him. This teaches us to refer ourselves to him. We do not know what is good for ourselves (Eccl. 6:12), but he knows what is good for us, so we must leave it up to him —*"Father, if you are willing... not my will, but yours, be done"* (Luke 22:42).

The child is supposed to ask for bread that he needs, and a fish, that is healthy; but if the child should foolishly ask for a stone, a snake, unripe fruit to eat, or a sharp knife to play with, the father, even though he is kind, is wise enough not to give those to him. We often ask God for things that would harm us if we had them. He knows this, and so does not give them to us. Denials in love are better than gifts in anger. We would be ruined if we had everything we wanted. A wise, non-Christian said it well:

Trust your fortune to the powers above. Leave them to manage it for you, and to give you what their perfect wisdom sees you need. In goodness and greatness, they excel. (Juvenal, Sat. 10).

Why He Gives

To encourage our prayers and expectations.

We hope we will not be denied and disappointed. We don't want a stone instead of bread to break our teeth, or a snake instead of a fish to bite us. There is enough reason for us to be afraid of this happening because we deserve it. But God will be better to us than the dessert of our sins. The world often gives stones for bread, and snakes for fish, but God never does. We will be heard and answered because that's what happens with children and their parents.

God has put a compassionate inclination into the hearts of parents to help and supply their children with everything they need. Even those that are not good at it, do it by instinct.

He has become a Father to us and taken us as his children. With the same tendency we have to look after our children, we can be encouraged to apply ourselves to him to look after us. The love and compassion fathers have are from him, not from nature but from the God of nature. So, the love and compassion must be much greater in him. He compares his concern for his people to that of a father for his children (Psalm 103:13), and even to that of a mother, which is usually more tender (Isa. 66:13-15).

His love, tenderness, and goodness are far more than those of any earthly parent. Therefore, it is clear and true that God is a better Father, way better than any earthly parents can be—his thoughts are above theirs (Isa. 55:9). Our earthly fathers have taken care of us, and we have taken care of our children. How much more will God take care of his own?

Earthly parents are born sinful and wicked, the seed of fallen Adam. They have lost much of the good nature that belonged to humanity, and among other things, have bad tempers and cruelty inside them, yet they give good things to their children, and they know how to give when the time is right. How much more will God do this, because when earthly parents abandon their children, he does not (Psalm 27:10).

First, God knows much more. Parents are often foolishly fond, but God is wise, he knows what we need, what we desire, and what is right for us. Secondly, God is much kinder. If all the compassions of all the fathers in the world were gathered into one man and compared with the tender mercies of God, they would be like a candle against the sun or a drop in the ocean. God is much richer and more ready to give to his children than earthly fathers can be. He is the Father of our spirits, an ever-loving, ever-living Father. The heart of the Father longs for his undutiful children, and is turned toward prodigal sons and daughters, as David's did for his son, Absalom—is this not enough to silence our disbelief?

Daily Reflection

The aspect of God as our Father is a key part of us becoming his children and understanding this relationship we have with him. Often, because of our earthly fathers, we do not always have a clear and perfect view of God in this way toward us. We have hurts, disappointments, and rejections to overcome before we can accept that God is truly our heavenly Father who wants the best for us. Coming to him in prayer in this way is essential. Asking him as a gracious father and expecting, as his children, that our prayers will become incredibly honest and trusting.

1. Why does Jesus use the example of our earthly fathers to describe how generous God is to us?
2. Do you find it easy or difficult to accept God as your Father?
3. What does the phrase "Denials in love are better than gifts in anger" mean?
4. Why will we be heard and answered as children?
5. Why does our Father in heaven want to give us good gifts?

2

THE HOLY SPIRIT HELPS US

For we do not know what to pray for as we ought, but the Spirit himself intercedes for us with groanings too deep for words.
Romans 8:26

While we are in this world, hoping and waiting for what we do not see, we must be praying. Hope requires desire, and that desire offered up to God is prayer—we groan. The Holy Spirit helps us in prayer:

Our weakness in prayer is that we do not know what we should pray for.

When it comes to our requests, we don't know what to ask. We are not good judges of our own condition. Who knows what is good for a person in this life? (Eccl. 6:12). We are short-sighted, very biased toward ourselves, and inclined to swap the means for the end. *"You do not know what you are asking"* (Matt. 20:22). We are like foolish children that ask for fruit before it is ripe and ready for them.

We also do not know the proper way or method to pray. It is not enough that we do what is good, we must do it well, and seek it at the right time. This is where we are often at a loss —characters are weak, emotions cold, thoughts wandering, and it is not always easy to find the heart to pray (2 Sam. 7:27). Paul speaks about this in the first person: *"We do not know."* He puts himself in with all the rest. Foolishness, weakness, and distraction in prayer are what all Christians complain about. If someone so great as Paul did not know what to pray for, how can we even think we can continue to do so in our own strength?

The Holy Spirit assists us in prayer. He helps our weaknesses, especially our praying weaknesses, which prevent us from doing it properly. The Spirit in our heart helps, living in us, working in us, as a Spirit of grace and supplication, especially when it comes to the weaknesses we suffer from when our faith is about to fail. This is why the Holy Spirit was poured out.

He helps us as we would help someone lift up a burden. He helps us—with us putting in our effort with the strength we have. We must not sit still and expect that the Spirit should do everything. When the Spirit goes before us we must motivate ourselves. We cannot do it without God, and he will not do it without us. What help does he give? The Spirit makes intercession for us, dictates our requests, writes our petitions, and composes our pleas for us. Christ intercedes for us in heaven, the Spirit intercedes for us in our hearts. This is how God has provided encouragement for praying Christians.

The Spirit, as an enlightening Spirit, teaches us what to pray for; as a sanctifying Spirit, works and stirs up praying character; as a comforting Spirit, silences our fears, and helps us over all our discouragements. The Holy Spirit is the spring of all our desires and words toward God.

Now, this intercession that the Spirit makes is:

With groanings that cannot be spoken. The strength and passion of those desires which the Holy Spirit works on is brought to life here. There can be praying in the Spirit where not one word is spoken, as Moses prayed (Exod. 14:15), and Hannah (1 Sam. 1:13). It is not the words and eloquence, but the faith and passion of our prayers that the Spirit works in us, as an intercessor. They cannot be spoken. They are so confused, the soul is so distracted with temptations and troubles, they do not know what to say, nor how to express themselves. Here is the Spirit interceding with groans that cannot be spoken. When we can only cry, "Abba, Father," and bring ourselves to him with humble boldness, this is the work of the Spirit.

According to the will of God (Rom. 8:27). The Spirit in the heart never contradicts the Spirit in the word. Those desires that are contrary to the will of God do not come from the Spirit. The Spirit interceding in us always melts our wills into the will of God. *"Not as I will, but as you will"* (Matt. 26:39).

The success of these intercessions is that the one who *"searches hearts knows what is the mind of the Spirit"* (Rom. 8:27). A hypocrite's religion lies in his tongue, nothing is worse than when God searches the heart and sees through all his disguises. For a sincere Christian who prays from his heart, nothing is more comfortable than when God searches the heart, for then he will hear and answer those desires which we want words to express. He *"knows what you need before you ask him"* (Matt. 6:8). He knows the mind of his own Spirit in us. And, as he always hears the Son interceding **for** us, so he always hears the Spirit interceding **in** us, because his intercession is according to the will of God.

What more could be done for the comfort of God's people, in all our addresses to God? Jesus said, *"Whatever you ask of the Father in my name, he will give it to you"* (John 16:23). How will we learn to ask according to his will? The Spirit will teach us that. Therefore, we will never seek in vain.

Daily Reflection

Without the Holy Spirit, our prayers suffer and die. They will be aimless arrows shot into the sky. Many times, we think we are able to do things in our own strength, especially when it comes to prayer, but eventually, we find that there is no other way but with the help of the Spirit. It is vital for us to acknowledge His role in prayer.

Even working through these daily reflection questions, ask the Holy Spirit to open your eyes to things you cannot and have not seen. It's His job to reveal and guide us to answers at the right time.

1. According to Henry, what is our weakness in prayer?
2. How does the Holy Spirit help us in these areas?
3. What are the groanings spoken of in Romans 8:26? Do you ever have those in your prayers?
4. How does the Spirit help us to pray according to God's will?
5. Why are our prayers effective and successful when we pray with the Spirit?

3

JESUS' PRAYER IN GETHSEMANE

Going a little farther he fell on his face and prayed, saying, "My Father, if it be possible, let this cup pass from me; nevertheless, not as I will, but as you will."
Matthew 26:39

Here we need to look at the following:

The place where he prayed. He went on by himself—*"Going a little farther"*—that the scripture might be fulfilled: "I have trodden the winepress alone" (Isa. 63:3). A troubled soul finds peace when it is alone with God, the one who understands the broken language of sighs and groans. Jesus teaches us here that secret prayer must be made secretly.

His posture in prayer. *"He fell on his face and prayed."* Lying on the ground shows:

The agony he was in, and how great his sorrow was. Job fell on the ground in great grief, and great anguish is expressed by rolling in the dust (Mic. 1:10).

His humility in prayer. This posture was an expression of his reverential fear (spoken of Hebrews 5:7), in the way he prayed.

The prayer itself. Here, we can see three things:

The title he gives to God. "*My Father.*" In all our addresses to God, we should see him as a Father, as our Father. Where should a child go when anything upsets him but his father?

The favor he asks. "*If it be possible, let this cup pass from me.*" He begs that this cup might pass from him—that he might avoid the sufferings before him or that they might be shortened. This is the first thing humans do is to pull back from anything harmful to us and to want it prevented or removed. Self-preservation is part of the nature of man, and rules until overruled by another law. So, Jesus admits and expresses a reluctance to suffer, to show he was human (Heb. 5:1), felt our weaknesses (Heb. 4: 15), and was tempted as we are but did not sin.

He says, "*If it be possible.*" If God might be glorified, man saved, and the result achieved, without his drinking the bitter cup, he would like it to be taken away, otherwise not.

His entire submission to the will of God. "*Nevertheless, not as I will, but as you will.*" Jesus, though he felt the extreme bitterness of the sufferings he was about to go through, was freely willing to submit to them for our redemption and salvation, and offered and gave himself for us. The reason for Jesus' submission was his Father's will—*"as you will."* His own willingness rest on the Father's will, therefore He did what He did, and did it joyfully because it was the will of God (Psalm 40:8). He often referred to this in his ministry: *"For this is the will of my Father"* (John 6:40). This he sought (John 5:30). It was his food to do it (John 4:34).

Following this example of Christ, we must drink of the bitter cup which God puts into our hands, no matter how bitter; even though we struggle against it, grace must submit. *"Let the will of the Lord be done"* (Acts 21:14).

The repetition of the prayer. *"Again, for the second time, he went away and prayed"* (Matt. 26:42), and again the third time (v. 44). Even though we pray to God to prevent and remove hardship, our main aim should be that He will give us the grace to endure it well. Prayer is offering up, not only our desires but our resignations, to God. This is all part of an acceptable prayer, when we are in distress, to bring ourselves to God, and to commit our way and work to Him: *"As you will."*

What answer did He receive to this prayer? The one that always heard Him, did not deny Him now. The cup did not go away from Him, but He had an answer to His prayer because He was strengthened with strength in his soul, on the day when He cried (Psalm 138:3), and that was a real answer (Luke 22:43). In answer to His prayer, God provided that He should not fail or be discouraged.

Daily Reflection

We often look at the things Jesus did as far above what we can ever go through or emulate. After all, He was God! And yet, as a human, He prayed just as we do. Jesus' prayer in the garden of Gethsemane is an especially emotional one. The agony and pain He exhibited while praying go beyond what most of us feel or endure when we come before God with our worries and needs. But that does not mean our prayers are any less effective or real to God. If we look at the different aspects of this prayer, we can see there are many parts to it that we also have in ours. We might not sweat drops like blood, but the manner in which we bring our hearts before God can be just as true.

1. Do you have a place to go and pray, somewhere far removed from everyone else?
2. What posture or position do you pray in? Do you think it's necessary to kneel or lie face down when we pray?
3. Look at Jesus' prayer; does yours follow His in any way? How?
4. Do you ever bring the same prayer to God again and again? Do you think it's necessary to repeat things we have already said?
5. What answer did Jesus receive to His prayer?

4

PRAYING IN SECRET

*But when you pray, go into your room and shut the door
and pray to your Father who is in secret.
And your Father who sees in secret will reward you.*
Matthew 6:6

"*And when you pray*" (Matt 6:5). It is taken for granted that all Christians pray. As soon as Paul was converted, he prayed. You cannot find a living man that does not breathe, just as you cannot find a living Christian that does not pray. Everyone that is godly prays. If you are prayerless, then you are graceless.

Not Like the Hypocrites

"*And when you pray, you must not be like the hypocrites*" (Matt 6:5). Those who don't want to act like hypocrites must not have the same attitude as hypocrites. It seems by reading

Matthew 23:13 that when Jesus talks of hypocrites, he means the scribes and Pharisees.

We must not be proud in prayer or look for the praise of people like the hypocrites. In all their acts of devotion, the main thing they wanted was to be commended by others, so they only did it for themselves. When it looked like their hearts were rising up in prayer, their eyes looked down on what they could get.

They prayed in the synagogues, which were good places for public prayer, but not for personal. They pretended to honor those places but only wanted to honor themselves. They prayed on the corners of the main streets where most people passed by and could hear what they said.

They prayed standing. This is not wrong—*"whenever you stand praying"* (Mark 11:25)—but kneeling is the more humble and reverent gesture (Luke 22:41, Acts 7:60, Eph. 3:14). The hypocrites stood because of the pride and confidence in themselves. The Pharisees stood and prayed (Luke 18:11).

They did not love prayer for itself, but they loved it when it gave them an opportunity to make themselves noticed. Sometimes our good deeds must be done publicly so others see them and commend them, but the sin and danger are when we love it and are pleased with it because it feeds our pride. The hypocrites wanted to be seen, not that God might accept them but that people might admire and applaud them.

This was their reward. They received everything they can expect from God for their service, and it is a poor repayment. What good is it to receive congratulations from people, if our

Master does not say, "Well done"? Those that want to approve themselves to God through their integrity in their faith must not look for the praise of people. It is not to people that we pray, nor do we expect an answer from them. They are not our judges, they are dust and ashes like us, and so we must not look to them. What goes on between God and our hearts must be out of sight. In our church worship, we must avoid everything that tends to make our personal devotion remarkable, like those that want their voices to be heard (Isa. 58:4). Public places are not right for private, solemn prayer.

Praying by Yourself

So, what does Jesus expect of us? Humility and sincerity. *"But when you pray"* go and do... (Matt. 6:6), specifically by yourself, and for yourself. Personal prayer is supposed to be the duty and practice of all Christians.

Instead of praying in the synagogues and on the corners of the streets, go into your room, into some place of privacy. Isaac went into the field (Gen. 24:63), Jesus to a mountain, and Peter to a housetop. No place of ceremony, as long as it meets the need. Secret prayer is to be done when we are alone, where we are not seen to avoid showing off; undisturbed to avoid distraction; unheard to have more freedom. But, if we cannot avoid being seen, we must not neglect the duty, because not praying at all would be even worse.

Instead of doing it to be seen by others, pray to your Father who is in secret. The Pharisees prayed to men rather than to God. Whatever they prayed, it was all for the applause of men, to gain their favor. "Well, you pray to God and that is enough for you. Pray to him as a Father, as your Father, ready to hear and answer, graciously ready to pity, help, and comfort you. Pray to your Father who is in secret." In secret prayer, we must keep our eyes on God who is present in all places. He is there in your room when no one else is there, very near to you when you call on him. In secret prayer, we give God the glory of his universal presence (Acts 17:24).

We are encouraged to pray like this because of the following:

Your Father sees in secret. He is looking to accept you when no one else is looking to applaud you. Jesus said to Nathaniel, *"Under the fig tree, I saw you"* (John 1:48). He saw Paul at prayer in a certain street, at a certain house (Acts 9:11). There is no secret, sudden breathing after God he does not see.

He will reward you openly. Those who pray openly receive their reward, and you will not lose yours for doing it in secret. It is called a reward, but it is from grace, not out of debt. The reward will be open. You will not only have it but have it honorably. The public reward is what the hypocrites want, but they don't have the patience to wait for it. Sometimes secret prayers are rewarded openly in this world; however, on the judgment day, there will be an open reward when all praying people will appear in glory with the great Intercessor. The Pharisees received their reward before all the people, and it was only a flash and shadow, but true Christians will have theirs before the whole world, the angels and people, and it will be glorious.

Daily Reflection

This is a crucial point that every other Puritan writer makes when talking about prayer. Secret, personal, private prayer is vital. There's a reason why Jesus talked about it and demonstrated it for His disciples to see. But there is also the danger of public, exposed prayer taking dominance in our lives because our pride always wants some type of recognition. It's why Jesus used this example when speaking about the two types of praying, warning us not to be hypocritical but to have a secure, personal prayer life.

1. Do you pray on your own, by yourself? How often do you do this?
2. Why is it so important to us and to God?
3. It speaks of the attitude of a hypocrite; what does that mean?
4. What happens when you have nowhere to go off by yourself to pray?
5. What is the reward Jesus is talking about here?

5

SHORT, SIMPLE PRAYERS

"And when you pray, do not heap up empty phrases as the Gentiles do, for they think that they will be heard for their many words. Do not be like them, for your Father knows what you need before you ask him."
Matthew 6:7-8

Even though the life of prayer is in lifting up the soul and pouring out the heart, there is a need for words in prayer, especially in public prayer. But Jesus warns us against being tempted to use language and expressions to show off and not to use useless repetitions when we're alone or with others. The Pharisees made long prayers, they made sure their prayers were long (Matt. 23:14).

No Useless Repetitions

The problem is making lip service of prayer, exercising the tongue, not the soul.

Useless repetitions—babbling over the same words again and again for no purpose. *"A fool multiplies words, though no man knows what is to be, and who can tell him what will be after him?"* (Eccl. 10:14). Not all repetition in prayer is condemned, just useless, self-centered repetitions. Jesus prayed, saying the same words (Matt. 26:44) out of passion (Luke 22:44). We see the same in Daniel 9:18-19. And there is an elegant repetition of the same words in Psalm 136. It is useful to express our emotions and to motivate others.

But the superstitious rehearsing of words, without thinking about them, like those who say so many Ave-Marias with their prayer beads; or the dry going over of the same things again and again, just to drill out the prayer to make it long, and show emotion when there is none—these are the vain repetitions condemned here. When we say a lot, but not much of it is purposeful, this is displeasing to God.

Lots of speaking, because of pride or superstition, or an opinion that God either needs to be informed or argued with by us, or out of foolishness, because people love to hear themselves talk. Not all long prayers are forbidden. Jesus prayed all night (Luke 6:12). Solomon's was a long prayer. Sometimes we need long prayers when the moment calls for it, but just prolonging the prayer, as if it would make it more pleasing to God, is condemned.

It is not praying a lot that is condemned, because we are told to always pray, but when we speak a lot. The danger of this is when we only say our prayers, and not when we pray them. This is explained by Solomon when he says, *"Therefore let your words be few"* (Eccl. 5:2). *"Take with you words"* (Hos. 14:2), *"choosing my words"* (Job 9:14). Do not say everything that comes into your mind.

Choose Your Words Carefully

The reasons against this are:

This is the way of the pagans, and it is not good for Christians to worship God that way. The pagans were taught by the light of nature to worship God. Thinking God was the same as them, they thought he needed many words to make him understand what was said to him or to make him answer their requests, as if he were weak and ignorant, and needed to be begged. It's why Baal's priests went from morning to night with their repetitions; *"O Baal, answer us!"*, but Elijah, with a very short prayer, was given fire from heaven, and then water (1 Kings 18:26, 36). Lip service in prayer, no matter how much effort is used, is worth nothing.

"Your Father knows what you need before you ask him," therefore there is no need for so many words. That does not mean you shouldn't pray, because God requires you by prayer to own your need for Him and dependence on Him and to please His promises. But you must state your case, pour out your hearts before Him, and then leave it with Him.

The God we pray to is our Father by creation and also by the new covenant in Christ Jesus. The way we speak to Him should be easy, natural, and unaffected. Children do not use to make long speeches to their parents when they want anything. Let us come to Him with the attitude of children, with love, reverence, and dependence. We will not need to say many words if we are taught by the Spirit of adoption to say "Abba, Father."

He is a Father that knows our case and knows our needs better than we do ourselves. He knows what we need. His eyes *"run to and fro throughout the whole earth,"* to see the needs of his people (2 Chron. 16:9), and He often gives before we call (Isa. 65:24), and more than we ask for (Eph. 3:20). If He does not give us what we ask, it is because He knows we do not need it, and that it is not for our good.

We don't need to be long or use many words in stating our case, God knows it better than we can tell Him, only He wants to hear it from us and then refer ourselves to Him, *"O Lord, all my longing is before you"* (Psalm 38:9). God is not moved by the length or language of our prayers. The most powerful intercessions are those made with groanings that cannot be spoken (Rom. 8:26). We are not to prescribe, but subscribe to God.

Daily Reflection

Henry was a very practical writer who used biblical authority to bring simple truths to his congregants and us. This chapter is straightforward. Even the heading says it all. Henry believed that short, simple prayers are safer and better when we come before God because it keeps us from wandering off the topic, getting caught up in our own words, and in our own thoughts. He does not just encourage us in praying simple, short prayers, but he backs them up with reasons.

1. Are your prayers long or short? Maybe ask someone else to tell you, because we can be biased toward what we think.
2. Why is lots of speaking in prayer not a good thing?
3. What is the difference between saying lots of words and persevering in prayer?
4. Why should we pray more like children speak to their parents?
5. If our Father knows what we need before we ask, why ask at all?

6

ASK, SEEK, AND KNOCK

*"Ask, and it will be given to you;
seek, and you will find;
knock, and it will be opened to you.
For everyone who asks receives, and the one who seeks finds,
and to the one who knocks it will be opened."*
Matthew 7:7-8

In Matthew 6, Jesus spoke of prayer as a commanded duty that honors God and is rewarded if done correctly. In Matthew 7, he speaks of it as the way for getting what we need, especially grace to obey the laws he had given.

The Command

To sum it up in three words: *"Ask… seek… knock…"* Basically, this means we must pray. Pray often. Pray with sincerity and seriousness. Pray, and pray again. Be mindful of prayer, and be constant in it. Make prayer your business, and be passionate about it. Ask, as a beggar asks for money. Those who want to be rich in grace must start begging, and they will be rewarded.

"*Ask.*" Bring your needs and burdens to God, and rely on him for support and supply, according to his promise. Ask as a traveler asks the way. To pray is to enquire of God (Ezek. 36:37).

"*Seek*" as if you are looking for something valuable you have lost, or as the trader seeks precious pearls. Seek by prayer (Dan. 9:3).

"Knock" as if you want to enter the house of the door you're knocking on. We will be admitted in to speak with God, taken into his love, favor, and kingdom. Sin has shut and locked the door. In prayer, we knock. Lord, open to us. Jesus knocks at our door (Rev. 3:20; Songs 5:2) and allows us to knock at his—something we don't even allow beggars to do.

Seeking and knocking imply something more than asking and praying.

We must not only ask, but seek. We must support our prayers with our efforts. We must seek the thing we ask for, or else we tempt God. When the owner of the vineyard asked for a year off for the barren fig tree, he added that he would dig and nurture it (Luke 13:7-8). God gives knowledge and grace to those who search the scriptures and wait at Wisdom's gates. He gives power against sin to those who avoid the moments they might happen.

We must not only ask, but knock. We must come to God's door and ask persistently. We must not only pray but plead and wrestle with God. We must seek diligently. We must continue knocking. We must persevere in prayer, and endure to the end in it.

The Promise

Here is an added promise: Our efforts in prayer will not be for nothing. When God finds a praying heart, he will be a prayer-hearing God. He will give you an answer of peace. It is a triple command: ask, seek, knock. It's a command on top of a command. The promise attached is sixfold, line upon line, for our encouragement, because believing in the promise makes us happy to continue in our obedience.

The promise is made to answer the command exactly:

"Ask, and it will be given to you"—not lent or sold to you, but given. What is better than a free gift? Whatever you pray for, according to the promise, whatever you ask, will be given to you if God decides it is good for you. What more do you need? Just ask and have. You don't have, because you don't have, or you don't ask correctly (James 4:3). What is not worth asking is not worth having, and then it is worth nothing.

"Seek, and you will find"—you will not lose your efforts. God is found by those who seek him, and if we find Him we have enough.

"Knock, and it will be opened to you"—the door of mercy and grace will not be closed as if you were an enemy or intruder,

but opened to you as friends and children. You will be asked who is at the door. If you can say, you are a friend and have the ticket of promise in the hand of faith, then do not doubt you will be let in. If the door is not opened at the first knock, continue in prayer. It is rude to knock at a friend's door and then go away. *"If it seems slow, wait for it"* (Hab. 2:3).

Daily Reflection

These daily reflections are for you to use at your own pace, at your own discretion, and in your own way. There is no rigid format or test to determine if you have answered correctly or not. Instead, each one will have questions that either relate to the passage in some way or lead you to think of what you have been reading for your own life. Some questions might seem personal, but it's for you—to see where you are in relation to what the Bible says, to see where you need some attention, and to see areas where you can grow.

1. What does Henry say when he says prayer is for getting "grace to obey the laws he had given"?
2. Why is seeking and knocking more than just asking?
3. How do we seek or knock when we are praying?
4. What are the promises attached to these three commands when we pray in this way?
5. What is your prayer life like? If you had to rate it out of 10 (10 being perfect), how would you fare?

7

WHAT IS PRAYER?

Hear my prayer, O LORD; give ear to my pleas for mercy!
Psalm 143:1

Prayer is an important part of religious worship that we are naturally drawn to and compelled to do by its basic laws. Pythagoras says, "Whatever men made a god of, they prayed to." Isaiah 44:17 also says, *"And the rest of it he makes into a god, his idol, and falls down to it and worships it. He prays to it and says, "Deliver me, for you are my god!"* Those who live without prayer live without God.

Prayer is the honest, religious acknowledgment of God and our desires. It's a sincere representation of holy emotions to give God the glory due to His name and to get the blessings He has promised, through the mediator, Jesus.

Our English word prayer is too simple, meaning petition or request, but humble adoration of God and thanksgiving are also necessary in prayer. The Greek word *Proseuche* is a vow to God. The Latin word *Votum* is used for prayer: The sailors on Jonah's ship made vows with their sacrifices—prayer is to move and oblige ourselves, not to move or oblige God.

Clemens Alexandrinus called prayer *Homilia pros ton Theon*—conversing with God. He shows that believers should live a life of communion with God, and so are always praying. They are people who, through prayer, continually converse with God. Some have specific hours of prayer, but a believer prays for his entire life. The Bible describes prayer as drawing near to God, lifting up our souls to Him, and pouring out our hearts before Him.

This is the life and soul of prayer. But this soul has a body, and that body must suit the soul, and adapt to it. Some words come from the mind in the same way smoke comes from incense. It's not so that God can understand us, because our thoughts are already known to Him, but that we may understand ourselves better.

A golden thread of heart-prayer must run through the web of our entire Christian lives. We must always be addressing ourselves to God in short and spontaneous prayers, keeping communion with God in our everyday actions as well as in religious services. So, prayer must be sprinkled into every duty, and our eyes must always be toward the Lord.

In mental prayer, thoughts are words—they are the product of the soul, dedicated to God. If it is better to focus our minds and motivate our devotions by giving words to our thoughts, and those thoughts are of the Spirit, the words will come. But if there are groanings that cannot be spoken in words, He that searches the heart knows them to be the mind of the Spirit and will accept them. *"And he who searches hearts knows what is the mind of the Spirit, because the Spirit intercedes for the saints according to the will of God. And we know that for those who love God all things work together for good, for those who are called according to his purpose"* (Romans 8:27-28).

He will answer the voice of our breathing (Lam. 3:56). But, because of the weakness of the flesh, and our hearts are inclined to wander, it's often necessary to first have words and be kept focused in our minds to the direction and motivation of holy emotions.

When we join with others in prayer, who are our mouths to God, our minds must join them, intelligently believing what they say, and our emotions, too. The Bible tells us to agree by saying "Amen," mentally if not vocally (1 Cor. 14:16). We can even join with our own words as long as they are in line and don't disrupt the prayer.

The person who is praying, whether in public or private, with the freedom of speech and holy liberty of prayer given to us, should not only check that it is for their own hearts but also for the encouragement of those who join them.

Daily Reflection

As Christians, many of us assume the duties set out before us without even asking why we are doing them. We go to church, read the Bible, and we pray. But what is prayer? This is a question many have asked, sometimes after years of being on their knees. What is prayer, and why do we even need it? Henry tackles this directly by giving us a detailed answer complete in Latin and Greek to substantiate his claims. Using a number of sources, he pulls together a complex answer to satisfy the query.

1. In your own words, how would you describe the act of praying?
2. Why do you think it is a necessary duty for us as Christians?
3. Why do you think God demands it of us?
4. Because it is a spiritual act, what role does Henry see the body playing?
5. Why do we need words in prayer if we have the Holy Spirit?

8

PSALM 17

I call upon you, for you will answer me, O God;
incline your ear to me; hear my words.
Psalm 17:6

The request of David's prayer is to experience the work of God in him, as evidence of and qualification for the goodwill of God toward him. This is grace and peace from God the Father.

He prays for the work of God's grace in him. *"My steps have held fast to your paths; my feet have not slipped"* (v. 5).

"Keep me steady in your paths. Lord, by your grace, I kept myself from the paths of the enemy. Keep me in your paths by the same grace. Let me not only be restrained from doing but quick to do good. Let my way be kept in your paths, so that I may not turn from them. Keep me in your paths, that I may not stumble and fall into sin, that I may not neglect my duty. Lord, as you have kept me this far, keep me still."

Those of us who are walking in God's paths need to pray, and do pray, that our way will be kept in those paths. We cannot stand any longer than He is pleased to hold us up, we can go no further than He is pleased to lead us, keep us up, and carry us. David had been kept in the way of his duty like this, and yet he does not think that this would be his security for the future, so he prays, *"Hold me up"* (Psalm 119:117). Those who would go in the way of God must, by faith and prayer, find grace and strength from Him every day. David knew that his way was slippery, that he was weak, and not as steady as he should be, that people were watching for him to fall, and so he prays, "Lord, hold me up, that my foot would not slip, that I may never say or do anything that is dishonest or distrustful."

He prays for signs of God's blessing to him. *"O Savior of those who seek refuge from their adversaries at your right hand"* (v. 7).

He sees God as the protector and savior of his people, so he calls Him, and finds encouragement from this in prayer: You who saves by your right hand—by your power, with no help from any other—those who trust you to keep them from their enemies.

It is the character of Christians that we trust in Him. He is pleased to make us confidants, for His secret is with the righteous. We trust Him because we commit ourselves to Him. Those who trust in God have many enemies, many rise up to ruin them, but they have one friend that is able to deal with them all, and, if He is for them, it does not matter who is against them (Rom. 8:31). It is His honor to be our savior. His almighty power works for us, and we have to see He is ready to save us. "You who saves those who trust in you from those that rise up against your right hand. Those that are enemies of Christians are rebels against God and his right hand, and surely he will eventually come against them."

The things he expects and desires from God: *"Wondrously show your steadfast love"* (v. 7). The word means special blessings. "Set apart your steadfast love for me. Do not just give me common blessings, but be gracious to me, as you do to those who love your name." It also means miraculous blessings. "Make your steadfast love worthy of praise! Lord, show your favor to me in such a way that I and others will be amazed by it." God's love is marvelous for the freedom and the fullness of it. Sometimes it shows itself in a special way: *"This is the LORD's doing; it is marvelous in our eyes"* (Psalm 118:23). This is especially true in the salvation of Christians when Jesus comes to be glorified in us and to be admired in all those who believe.

Daily Reflection

Many of the psalms feature David calling for help from his enemies, asking God for protection against them, and for judgment to come on them. It's easy to flip over to another psalm because we think these don't apply to us. We're not royalty with people plotting our downfall or kingdoms trying to uproot us. And yet, the basic premise is that we face the same issues as David. There are always those who don't agree with us; they don't have our best interests at heart or oppose us because of our faith. We need the Lord just as much as David did.

1. What do grace and keeping us steady have in common?
2. Do you ever pray the same type of prayer as he did: "Hold me up"?
3. Do you think it's right to pray for judgment on those who are your enemies?
4. Why is Romans 8:31 such a powerful verse to remember and to use in our prayers?
5. How does God show his steadfast love through us?

9

PRAYING FOR PROTECTION FROM OTHERS

*Keep me as the apple of your eye;
hide me in the shadow of your wings.*
Psalm 17:8

Let us look at what David prays for: Being surrounded by enemies that threatened his life, he prays for God to preserve him safely through all their attempts against him. This prayer is a pattern for Christians to bring their souls so God can keep them.

He prays for protection. *"Keep me as the apple of your eye; hide me in the shadow of your wings"* (v. 8). "Keep me safe, hide me close, where I will not be found by others. Deliver my soul, not only my physical life from death but my spirit from sin." Those who put themselves under God's protection can find the benefit of it in faith.

If we keep God's law as the apple of our eye (Prov. 7:2), we can expect God to keep us because whoever touches God's people, touches the apple of his eye (Zech. 2:8). Jesus uses the example of keeping us safe under his wings (Matt. 23:37). "Hide me under the shadow of your wings, where I will be safe and warm."

David prays, "Lord, keep me *'from the wicked who do me violence, my deadly enemies who surround me.'"* (v. 9) "Keep me from being destroyed by them. Let them not have their way against me or triumph over me."

He prays that all the plans of his enemies to pull him into sin or trouble will be defeated: *"Arise, O LORD! Confront him, subdue him! Deliver my soul from the wicked by your sword"* (v. 13). How many times did Saul miss his target when he persecuted David? How disappointed were Jesus' enemies by his resurrection, when they thought they had made their point by putting him to death?

He pleads his own dependence on God as his portion and happiness. *"As for me, I shall behold your face in righteousness; when I awake, I shall be satisfied with your likeness"* (v. 15).

"The wicked have their portion in this life, but 'as for me,' I am not like them, I do not have much in this world—I neither have, need, nor care for it. It is the vision and fulfillment of God that I place my happiness in. That is what I hope for. This is what sets me apart and distinguishes me from those who have their reward in this life."

Seeing God's face is what brings us satisfaction.

This is our duty and happiness in this world. In righteousness—clothed with Jesus' righteousness, having a good heart and a good life—by faith we see God's face and always have Him before us. This is how we satisfy ourselves every day, with the contemplation of the beauty of the Lord. When we wake up every morning, we must be satisfied with the image of himself He has shown us in the Bible, and with His image on us through His renewing grace. Our experience of God's blessing, and our conformity to Him, should bring us more satisfaction than those whose stomachs are filled with delicacies.

It is our reward and happiness in the spirit. It is the same prayer he ends the previous Psalm with: *"You make known to me the path of life; in your presence there is fullness of joy; at your right hand are pleasures forevermore"* (Psalm 16:11). That joy is prepared and designed only for the righteous who are justified and sanctified. We will have it when we die: when our souls wake up out of their sleep in the body, and when our bodies wake up, at the resurrection, out of their sleep in the grave.

That wonderful moment will consist of three things:

We will see God and his glory. I will see your face, not as in this world, as *"in a mirror dimly"* (1 Cor. 13:12). The knowledge of God will be perfected there.

We will resemble him. Our holiness will be perfect there. This will be a result of seeing him: *"When he appears we shall be like him, because we shall see him as he is"* (1 John 3:2).

We will be completely content. I will be satisfied, abundantly satisfied. There is no satisfaction for a soul except in God, and in His face and image, His goodness toward us, and His good work in us. That satisfaction will not be perfect until we get to heaven.

Daily Reflection

Have a notebook handy when you are reading through Matthew Henry's words. Make notes of anything that stands out to you so you can remember them. Write down anything that comes to mind as you're working through the reflection questions. Remember, these are just a guide to get you thinking more about prayer and how it pertains to your own life. By keeping a journal, you can keep track of your thoughts and answers. Also, take note of any specific verses that may jump out at you.

1. What is the "apple of your eye"? Why is that what we want to be to God?
2. What kind of deliverance is David praying for here?
3. What does it mean to see God's face? Why is this important for Christians?
4. Read Psalm 27:8. What does this verse mean?
5. What does it mean to be complete and satisfied in God?

10

THE LORD'S PRAYER (PREFACE)

"Our Father in heaven."
Matthew 6:9

The preface: *"Our Father in heaven."* Before we get to our business, there must be a respectful address to the one we will be dealing with—our Father. We announce that we must pray, not only alone and for ourselves, but with and for others, because we are members together, and are called into fellowship with each other. Jesus teaches us to whom we pray, only to God—not to saints and angels, because they know nothing of us, should not be given any honor in prayer, and can give none of the blessings and favors we expect. We are taught how to address ourselves to God, and what title to give him, a title that says He is not just majestic, but generous and kind, because we must come boldly to the throne of grace (Heb. 4:16).

We must come before Him as our Father, and call Him by this name. He is a Father to all people by creation (Mal. 2:10, Acts 17:28). In a special way, He is a Father to Christians, by adoption and regeneration (Eph. 1:5, Gal. 4:6), and what an incredible privilege it is. This is how we must see Him in prayer, and continue thinking of Him, so we are encouraged and not afraid. There is nothing more pleasing to God or ourselves, than to call God Father. When Jesus prayed, He often called God Father.

If He is our Father, He will have compassion on our weaknesses (Psalm 103:13), will show us mercy (Mal. 3:17), will make the best of our performances, and will not hold back anything that is good for us (Luke 11:11-13). We have confident access to Him, as to a father, and have an advocate with the Father, and the Spirit of adoption. When we repent of our sins, we must see God as a Father, as the prodigal did (Luke 15:18, Jer. 3:19). When we beg for grace, peace, and the inheritance of children, it is encouraging to come to God, not as an unreconciled, hostile judge but as a loving, gracious, reconciled Father in Christ (Jer. 3:4).

As He is our Father in heaven, He is also everywhere else, because heaven cannot contain Him. But it is in heaven that His glory is shown, because it is His throne (Psalm 103:19), and to us believers, it is a throne of grace. So, that is where we must direct our prayers, because Jesus the Mediator is now in heaven—"*We have such a high priest, one who is seated at the right hand of the throne of the Majesty in heaven*" (Heb. 8:1). We cannot see heaven or the world of spirits, so when we speak to God in prayer, it must be spiritual. Therefore, in prayer we must be raised above the world, and lift up our hearts (Psalm 5:1). Heaven is a place of perfect purity, so we must lift up pure hands and learn to sanctify His name, the Holy One, who lives in that holy place (Lev. 10:3).

"The LORD looks down from heaven; he sees all the children of man; from where he sits enthroned he looks out on all the inhabitants of the earth" (Psalm 33:13-14). In prayer, we must see that He is looking down at us. He has a full and clear view of all our needs, burdens, desires, and weaknesses. As a Father He is not only able to help us, or do great things for us, more than we can ask or think, He can supply our needs, for every good gift is from above. He is a Father, so we can come to Him with boldness. But He is a Father in heaven, so we must also come with reverence (Eccl. 5:2).

All our prayers should be in line with our great aim as Christians—to be with God in heaven. God and heaven, the end of our whole conversation, must be our focus in every prayer. That is the center of everything. By prayer, we send everything before us to heaven, where we are also going one day. And, since heaven is our Father's house, we may speak there, and seek the things that are above (John 14:2, Phil. 3:20, Col. 3:1).

Help us to come to you with humble boldness and confidence, as we would to a Father, a tender Father, who spares us as a man spares his son that serves him. We have an advocate with the Father, who has told us that the Father loves us (Eph. 3:12, Mal. 3:17, 1 John 2:1, John 16:27).

You are our Father in heaven, so we lift up our souls to you. We lift up our eyes to you who live in the heavens. As the eyes of a servant look on his master's hand, so our eyes wait on you, Lord. You are a God whom the heavens cannot contain, and yet we have access to you, having a high priest who has gone up into heaven before us (Psalm 86:4, Psalm 123:1-2, 1 Kings 8:27, Eph. 3:12, Heb. 4:14, Heb. 6:20).

Daily Reflection

It's no surprise that the Lord's Prayer is featured in a book about prayer. As one of the most pivotal moments of Jesus' teaching, it stands out. But because of its significance, it's almost been elevated to a super-spiritual prayer rather than what Jesus intended it to be—an example or a format for our own prayers. Instead of learning and saying the words verbatim, without any meaning, this prayer is meant to be a pattern to follow, an order on which we can base our own words and thoughts toward God. Henry breaks this pattern down for us, verse by verse.

1. Have you ever said the Lord's Prayer aloud in church? What was the occasion?
2. Do you think it has lost its meaning over the years?
3. Why is it so important to begin our prayers in the right way, rather than beginning with our wants and needs?
4. Do you think it's significant that God is addressed here as "our Father," and not one of his other many titles?

11

THE LORD'S PRAYER (FIRST PETITIONS)

Hallowed be your name.
Your kingdom come,
your will be done,
on earth as it is in heaven."
Matthew 6:9-10

There are six petitions in the Lord's Prayer. The first three relate to God and his honor, the last three to our own concerns, both physical and spiritual. It's the same as in the ten commandments, the first four teach us our duty toward God, and the last six our duty toward our neighbor. The method of this prayer teaches us to seek first the kingdom of God and his righteousness, and then to hope that other things shall be added.

"Hallowed be your name." It is the same word as sanctified. It's used here because people were used to it in the Lord's prayer, in these words.

We give glory to God. It is not a petition, but an adoration, because the Lord is magnified, or glorified—God's holiness is the greatness and glory of all His perfections. We must begin our prayers with praising God, and it is right that He should be served first, and that we should give glory to God before we expect to receive mercy and grace from Him. Let Him receive praise for his perfections, and then let us have the benefit of them.

We must get our part right, and it should be our main and ultimate goal in all our petitions, that God may be glorified. All our other requests must come second to this, and follow after. "Father, glorify yourself in giving me my daily bread and forgiving my sins," etc. Since everything is from Him and through Him, everything must be to Him and for Him. In prayer our thoughts and love should be to the glory of God. The Pharisees made their own name the main part of their prayers (Matt. 6:5) instead of making the name of God the goal. Let all our petitions center on this and be ruled by it.

We desire and pray that the name of God, in everything that He has made himself known, may be sanctified and glorified by us and others, and especially by himself. "Father, let your name be glorified as a Father, and a Father in heaven. Glorify your goodness, majesty, and mercy. Let your name be sanctified, because it is a holy name. No matter what happens to our polluted names, but Lord, what will you do for your great name?" When we pray that God's name is glorified,

We show necessity—God will sanctify his own name, whether we want it or not. *"I will be exalted among the nations"* (Psalm 46:10).

We ask for something that will definitely be given—when Jesus prayed, *"Father, glorify your name"* (John 12:28), it was immediately answered, *"I have glorified it, and I will glorify it again."*

"Your kingdom come." This petition is what Jesus preached during His ministry, what John Baptist preached before that, and what He sent his apostles out to preach after He left—*"The kingdom of heaven is at hand"* (Matt. 4:17). The kingdom of your Father who is in heaven, the kingdom of the Messiah, this is available, pray that it may come. We should turn the word we hear into prayer, our hearts should echo it. Does Jesus promise to come soon? Our hearts should answer, "Yes, come." Ministers should pray over the word. When they preach, the kingdom of God is at hand, they should pray, Father, *"Your kingdom come."* What God has promised, we must pray for, because promises are given to motivate and encourage prayer. When the accomplishment of a promise is about to happen, when the kingdom of heaven is at hand, we should pray for it even more, *"Your kingdom come."*

It's the same as when Daniel prayed for the deliverance of Israel, when he understood that the time of it was near (Dan. 9:2). Look at Luke 19:11. It was the Jews' daily prayer to God, "Let him make his kingdom reign, let his redemption flourish, and let his Messiah come and deliver his people." Let your kingdom come, let the gospel be preached to all and embraced by all. Let everyone be brought to believe the account God has given in His word about his Son, and to embrace Him as their Savior and King. Let the boundaries of the church be enlarged, the kingdom of the world be made Christ's kingdom, and all people become subjects to it, and live according to it.

"Your will be done, on earth as it is in heaven." We pray that as God's kingdom comes, we and others will be obedient to all its laws. Then we will see that Jesus' kingdom is here. Let God's will be done, and we will see the kingdom of heaven has come, let it introduce a heaven on earth. Jesus will only be a puppet-prince if we call him King and do not do his will. If we pray that He may rule us, we pray that in everything we will be ruled by Him.

When we pray *"Your will be done,"* we say, "Lord, do what you want with me and mine (1 Sam. 3:18). I bring myself to you, and am satisfied that everything you say about me should be done." This is how Jesus prayed, *"Not my will, but yours, be done"* (Luke 22:42). "Help me to do what is pleasing to you. Give me the necessary grace to know your will, and be obedient to it. Let your will be done by me and others—not our own will, of the flesh, the mind, or of people (1 Pet. 4:2), and not Satan's will (John 8:44)—that we may not anger God in anything we do or be displeased by anything God does."

Daily Reflection

The words of this prayer often trip off our lips without us actually realizing their full meaning, especially when it includes old, antiquated words like "hallowed." We say it, knowing it is something important and great, but it is done more in routine than with heart and knowledge. Henry's methodical approach in stripping the Lord's Prayer down line by line is useful for us to come back to its full explanation. Seeing the format of petitions adds great importance to it as an example for us.

1. What does *"hallowed"* mean? Why is it important to start in this attitude?
2. Why does the Lord's Prayer begin with petitions to God's honor before our own needs?
3. What is meant by the words *"your kingdom come"*?
4. What is God's will that we pray about here?
5. Look through the psalms and see if you can find a similar format, where the prayers begin with praise and honor before getting down to our own needs and wants.

12

THE LORD'S PRAYER (SECOND PETITIONS)

> *"Give us this day our daily bread,*
> *and forgive us our debts,*
> *as we also have forgiven our debtors.*
> *And lead us not into temptation,*
> *but deliver us from evil."*
> Matthew 6:11-13

There are six petitions in the Lord's Prayer. The first three relate to God and his honor, the last three to our own concerns, both physical and spiritual.

"Give us this day our daily bread." Because our natural being is necessary to our spiritual well-being in this world, after God's glory, kingdom, and will, we pray for the necessary provisions and comforts of this present life. These are the gifts of God, and must be asked of Him—bread for the approaching day, for the rest of our lives. Bread for the time

to come, or bread for our being and subsistence in the world (Prov. 30:8), food convenient for us and our families.

Every word here has a lesson:

We ask for **bread**—that teaches us moderation and self-control. We ask for bread—not delicacies, not excess—only what is healthy, even though it may not be nice.

We ask for **our** bread—that teaches us honesty and industry. We do not ask for the bread out of other people's mouths—not the bread of deceit (Prov. 20:17), not the bread of laziness (Prov. 31:27)—but bread gained honestly.

We ask for our **daily** bread—that teaches us not to think about tomorrow (Matt. 6:34), but to constantly depend on divine provision, like those who live from hand to mouth.

We beg God to **give** it to us—not sell it to us, nor lend it to us, but give it. Even the greatest people must depend on the mercy of God for their daily bread.

We pray, "Give it to **us**. not only to me, but to others like me." This teaches us charity and a compassionate concern for the poor and needy. It also means that we should pray with our families—we eat together, therefore we should pray together.

We pray that God would give us **this day**—that teaches us to renew the desire of our souls toward God, as the needs of our bodies are renewed. As the day comes, we must pray to our heavenly Father, and realize we could go without food for a day, if we go without prayer.

"And forgive us our debts, as we also have forgiven our debtors." This is connected with the petition before. *"And forgive"* means that unless our sins are pardoned, we can have no comfort in life, or the provision of it. Our daily bread only feeds us like lambs for slaughter if our sins are not pardoned. It also means that we must pray for daily forgiveness, just as we pray for daily bread. Here is:

A petition. Father in heaven, forgive us our debts, our debts to you. Our sins are our debts. There is a debt of duty, which we owe to our Creator as creatures. For not observing the law, we stand under the penalty. An offender is a debtor to the law, so are we. Our hearts' desire and prayer to our heavenly Father every day should be that He would forgive us our debts. That the punishment may be canceled, that we may not be condemned, that we may be released. In asking for forgiveness of our sins, the plea we have to rely on is Jesus' death satisfied the justice of God for the sin of man, he became our guarantee.

An argument to enforce this petition. *"As we also have forgiven our debtors."* This is not a plea of merit, but a plea of grace. Those who come to God for the forgiveness of their sins against him must forgive those who have offended them; otherwise, they curse themselves when they say the Lord's prayer. Our duty is to forgive our debtors. We must forgive and forget the wrongs against us. This is a moral qualification for pardon and peace. It encourages hope in us that God will forgive us. If there is this gracious attitude in us, it is from God—evidence that He has forgiven us, having formed the condition of forgiveness in us.

"And lead us not into temptation, but deliver us from evil." This petition is expressed:

Negatively. *"Lead us not into temptation."* Having prayed that the guilt of sin may be removed, we pray that we may never return to it again, that we may not be tempted to it. God did not tempt anyone to sin, but we say, "Lord, do not let Satan loose on us, chain up that roaring lion, because he is sneaky and spiteful. Lord, do not leave us to ourselves (Psalm 19:13), because we are weak. Lord, do not put obstacles and traps before us, nor circumstances that can cause us to fall." Temptations must be prayed against, because of the discomfort and trouble of them, and because of the danger of being overcome by them, and the guilt and grief that follow.

Positively. *"But deliver us from evil."* From the evil one, the devil, the tempter. "Keep us, so that we may not be attacked by him, or overcome by those attacks. Lord, deliver us from the evil of the world, the corruption that is in the world through lust. Keep us from the evil of every condition in the world, from the evil of death. Deliver us from ourselves, from our own evil hearts. Deliver us from evil men, that they may not be a trap to us, and we will not be a prey to them."

Daily Reflection

We all have our lists that we bring before God, ticking off all the important boxes to make sure our every need is met, and our desires are taken into consideration! In fact, sometimes the majority of our prayers are made up of requirements. It's interesting how Jesus summed everything up into just a few lines, and instead of going into specifics, he rolls all our concerns into three petitions. Henry shows us just how incredible these requests are by analyzing each one and dissecting them for deeper meaning.

1. Do you think it's necessary to pray for our basic needs every day?
2. Which part of *"give us this day our daily bread"* speaks to you the most after seeing it broken down by Henry?
3. Why is it important to pray for forgiveness?
4. Do you find God answers you if and when you pray against temptations?
5. Doesn't God protect us from Satan without us having to ask him to do so?

13

THE LORD'S PRAYER (CONCLUSION)

"For thine is the kingdom, and the power, and the glory, for ever. Amen."
Matthew 6:13 (KJV)

Some link the end of the Lord's Prayer to David's doxology in 1 Chronicles 29:11: *"Yours, O LORD, is the greatness and the power and the glory and the victory and the majesty, for all that is in the heavens and in the earth is yours. Yours is the kingdom, O LORD, and you are exalted as head above all."*

David adores God and ascribes glory to him as the God of Israel, blessed forever and ever. This is properly praising God —with holy awe and reverence, and love. He acknowledges:

His infinite characteristics. Not only that He is great, powerful, glorious, etc., but that the greatness, power, and glory are His—He has them in and of himself. He is the fountain and center of everything that is bright and blessed. His is the greatness. His greatness is immense and incomprehensible. All others are little, and are nothing, in comparison to Him. His is the power, and it is almighty and irresistible. Power belongs to Him, and all the power of all the creatures comes from Him and depends on Him. His is the glory. His glory is His own end and the end of the whole creation. All the glory we can give Him with our hearts, lips, and lives come very short of what is due to Him. His is the victory. He is above all and is able to conquer and subdue all things to himself. And His is the majesty, real and personal. With Him is terrible majesty, inexpressible and inconceivable.

His sovereign dominion, as rightful owner of all. "All that is in heaven and earth is yours, and is at your disposal, because you created it. As supreme ruler and commander of everything, yours is the kingdom, and all kings are your subjects, because you are head, and are to be exalted and worshiped as head above all."

His universal influence. All that is rich and honorable among the children of men have their riches and honors from God. All princes receive their riches and honor from Him, and what they give back is only a small part of what they had received from Him. Whoever is great is because God makes them so, and whatever strength we have, God gives it to us (Psalm 68:35).

The Lord's prayer is similar but has three parts:

A plea to enforce the petitions that came before in the prayer. It is our duty to plead with God in prayer, to fill our mouths with arguments (Job 23:4). These arguments are not to move God, but to affect ourselves—to encourage our faith, to excite our passion. Now, the best pleas in prayer are those that are taken from God himself, from what He has made known of himself. We must wrestle with God in our pleas.

Here, there is a special reference to the first three petitions in the prayer "Father in heaven, your kingdom come, for yours is the kingdom. Your will be done, for yours is the power. Hallowed be your name, for yours is the glory." This is encouraging for us in our own tasks. "Yours is the kingdom—you have the government of the world, and the protection of Christians in it." God gives and saves like a king. "Yours is the power—to maintain and support that kingdom, and to meet the needs of your people." "Yours is the glory—the end of all that is given and done for Christians, in answer to their prayers." This is a matter of comfort and holy confidence in prayer.

It is a form of praise and thanksgiving. The best pleading with God is praising Him. It is the way to get more mercy, as it qualifies us to receive it. In all our addresses to God, it is right that there should be a lot of praise because praise suits Christians. It is just and equal: We praise God, and give Him glory, not because He needs it—He is praised by angels—but because He deserves it. It is our duty to give Him glory, in the way He created and revealed himself to us. Praise is the work and happiness of heaven. Everyone who wants to go to heaven must begin their heaven now.

See how complete this doxology is: "The kingdom, and the power, and the glory, it is all yours." It suits us to praise God a lot. A true Christian never thinks they can give God enough glory. There should be gracious fluency in this forever.

Ascribing glory to God forever shows an acknowledgment that it is eternally due, and a desire to be doing it eternally with the angels and saints above (Psalm 71:14).

Lastly, we are taught to add our *"Amen"*—so be it. God's Amen is permission—his command is, it will be so. Our Amen is only a desire—our command is, let it be so. It is in the token of our desire and assurance to be heard, that we say Amen. Amen refers to every petition going before, and so, in compassion for our weaknesses, we are taught to sum up everything in one word, so that we don't leave anything out. It is good to end religious duties with some passion and energy, so that we may leave uplifted in our spirits. Long ago, people said "Amen" out loud at the end of every prayer, and this is good, as long as it is said with understanding, as Paul directs (1 Cor. 14:16), and our inner expressions agree with our outward expression of desire and confidence.

Daily Reflection

We spend a lot of time being concerned with the beginning and the content of our prayers without paying much attention to the end. Our modern prayers end when we run out of words or we finish bringing our list to God, then we wrap it up by saying, "Amen." We seem to have lost some of the etiquette and understanding from the past, where it was expected to thank and praise God as we conclude what we have brought before the Lord. Henry sees the importance of this and does not rush through his words as he emphasizes it for our own prayers.

1. Do you think we need to honor God again at the end of a prayer if we have already done so in the beginning?
2. What does Henry mean by saying, "the best pleading with God is praising him"?
3. Do you praise God often? Do you find it easy to do?
4. What do you understand in saying the word "Amen" at the end of a prayer?
5. What is the end of your prayers like? Maybe ask someone else to get an unbiased point of view.

14

A METHOD FOR PRAYER

In God, whose word I praise,
in the LORD, whose word I praise.
Psalm 56:10

It is best to have many full prayers. Our burdens, worries, and needs are many, and so are our sins and mercies. The promises are numerous and very rich, our God gives generously, and tells us to *"Open your mouth wide, and I will fill it"* (Psalm 81:10). He will satisfy us with good things. We are not limited in Him, so why should we be limited in our spirits? Jesus taught His disciples the Lord's prayer but said to them, *"Until now you have asked nothing in my name"* (John 16:24). They asked nothing compared to what they should ask when the Spirit should be poured out. Then He says, *"Ask, and you will receive, that your joy may be full."* We are encouraged to be specific in prayer, and in everything to make our requests known to God, as we should also be specific in the worship of God's attributes, in the confession of our sins, and in our thankful acknowledgments of God's mercies.

There needs to be some method used in prayer, not only to say the right things but that they are said in their proper place and time—that we don't bring anything confusing or out of line. We must be careful not to be careless with our mouth, nor too quick to say anything before God—not to say the first thing that comes to us, nor mindlessly repeat words that do not show passion but emptiness. The matters we bring to God are important, and we should check our words, that they are well-chosen and well-placed.

Just as it is good to be methodical in prayer, it is also good to be instructive. The Lord's Prayer, David's psalms, and many of Paul's prayers are good examples.

When it comes to the words and expressions we use in prayer, even though we should use scriptural language, because the Bible is enough to help us in everything, it is convenient and often necessary to use other expressions in prayer besides those that are purely biblical. I would advise that the scriptural words are used most of the time and become familiar to us and others when we engage in holy things. It's the language Christians are most accustomed to, most affected with, and will most readily agree to. When the Bible is opened and explained, scriptural language will be most intelligible, and the meaning understood. This is good, solid speech that cannot be condemned. It is good to paraphrase the verses, still speaking according to scriptural rules, comparing spiritual things with spiritual.

Even though I recommend using biblical words as a good method for prayer, I do not think we should always tie ourselves to it. It is good to have variations and different expressions. Thanksgiving can sometimes come before confession or petition, or our intercessions for others before our petitions for ourselves, as in the Lord's prayer. Sometimes we can spend more time on one of these parts of prayer than another, or they can be interwoven.

There are those who sometimes are so full and lifted up in their hearts in prayer, they are so focused in their thoughts, and have such passion in holy emotions, the product is a fluency and variety of relevant and moving words that come naturally, that to use a method or structure would be a hindrance to them and would cramp and limit them. This does not always happen, and there is a need to have a certain method to follow in prayer so that it can be done properly and orderly, as long as it does not become too formal. A person can write straight without having his paper ruled.

But in the end, the intentions and thoughts of the mind, the passionate display of faith and love, and the holy desire toward God are so essentially necessary to prayer, that without these in sincerity, the best and most proper language is just a lifeless image. *"If I speak in the tongues of men and of angels, but have not love, I am a noisy gong or a clanging cymbal"* (1 Cor. 13:1). It is only the effective, passionate prayer, the formed-in-us, born-in-us prayer, that succeeds. So, we should approve ourselves to God in the integrity of our hearts, whether we pray with a pre-written form or without it.

Daily Reflection

Taken from Henry's book, *A Method for Prayer,* this reading is part of his introduction, explaining the need and effectiveness of using proper words to direct us. Too many times, people begin with an idea then spontaneously follow their thoughts, thinking it's the Holy Spirit. These often become meandering diatribes! By using the Bible as a base, we can bring our ideas and words in line with what God says. In his book, Henry compiles many prayers using scripture, and it will benefit your prayer life incredibly if you borrow from this treasure trove. You can find this book in shops or online (a newer edition is titled *"Learn to Pray the Bible"*).

1. What is your view of spontaneous prayer compared to using some type of format or verse to guide you?
2. Why do you think it is good to be specific in prayer, according to Henry?
3. What does Henry say is essentially necessary for prayer?
4. Have you ever used words from the Bible while you are praying, perhaps paraphrasing them? Did it help at all?
5. What is meant by a "formed-in-us, born-in-us" prayer?

15

BRING EVERYTHING TO GOD IN PRAYER

Do not be anxious about anything, but in everything by prayer and
supplication with thanksgiving
let your requests be made known to God.
Philippians 4:6

Paul begins the chapter of Philippians by encouraging the Christians in their duties:

He encourages us in mutual assistance: *"I entreat Euodia and I entreat Syntyche to agree in the Lord"* (v. 2-3). Sometimes we need to apply the general precepts of the gospel from specific cases like this. Paul says, "Pray to be of the same mind in the Lord, to keep the peace and live in love, to be of the same mind one with another, not contradicting, and to be of the same mind with the rest of the church, not acting in opposition to them."

He encourages us to have holy joy and delight in God: *"Rejoice in the Lord always; again I will say, rejoice"* (v. 4). All our joy must be found in God, and our thoughts of God must be wonderful thoughts. *"Delight yourself in the LORD"* (Psalm 37:4). In all our thoughts (terrible, hurtful thoughts) his *"consolations cheer my soul"* (Psalm 94:19). And our *"meditation be pleasing to him"* (Psalm 104:34).

It is our duty and privilege to rejoice in God and to rejoice in him always. At all times, in all conditions, even when we suffer for him. We must not think badly of him or his ways because of the hardships we face while serving him. There is enough in God to bring us joy in the worst circumstance on earth. Paul said it before: *"Finally, my brothers, rejoice in the Lord"* (Phil. 3:1). Here he says it again, *"Rejoice in the Lord always; again I will say, rejoice."* Joy in God is an important duty in the Christian life. Christians need to be reminded of it again and again. If good men do not have a continual feast, it is their own fault.

We are encouraged to be honest and gentle, and gracious toward others: *"Let your reasonableness be known to everyone"* (v. 5). In everyday things do not swing to extremes; avoid prejudices and animosity; judge graciously concerning one another. The Greek word here is *epieikes*, which means a good attitude toward other people—it is explained in Romans 14. It's understood as being patient in hardship or enjoying things in moderation. This links in with the next verse because Jesus is coming soon.

Here is a warning against worrying (v. 6): *"Do not be anxious about anything"*— the same expression found in Matthew

6:25, *"Do not be anxious about your life"*—avoid worrying distracting thoughts about the needs and difficulties of life. It is the duty and interest of Christians to live without worrying. There is a concern of being diligent which is our duty, being wise in looking ahead, but there is a care of mistrust which is sin and foolishness, and which only perplexes and distracts the mind. Worry about nothing, because not trusting God will make you unfit for his service.

As a cure against anxious worrying, Paul recommends we stay in constant prayer: *"In everything by prayer and supplication with thanksgiving let your requests be made known to God"* (v. 6).

Here we must see the following:

We must not only have regular times for prayer, but we must pray in every specific emergency: *"In everything by prayer."* When anything burdens our spirits, we must ease our minds with prayer. When events become confusing or distressing, we must look for direction and support.

We must add thanksgiving to our prayers and supplications. *"With thanksgiving."* We must not only look for good things but own receipts of mercy. Grateful acknowledgments of what we have show a good attitude, and are effective motives for further blessings.

Prayer is offering up our desires to God, making them known to him: *"Let your requests be made known to God."* Not that God needs to be told our needs or desires, because he knows them better than we can tell him, but he wants to know them from us, and for us to bring our thoughts and concern to him, express how much we value his mercy and are dependent on him.

The result of this will be the peace of God keeping our hearts (v. 7). *"The peace of God"* is the sense of our reconciliation to God and interest in his favor, and the hope of enjoying God in heaven one day, *"which surpasses all understanding,"* is something that can be properly valued and expressed. It has not yet entered into the heart of man (1 Cor. 2:9). This peace will keep our hearts and minds through Christ Jesus. It will keep us from sinning in hard times, and from sinking under them. It will keep us calm and sedate, without confusion, and with inner satisfaction. *"You keep him in perfect peace whose mind is stayed on you"* (Isa. 26:3).

In these things, Paul shows himself to them as an example: *"What you have learned and received and heard and seen in me—practice these things, and the God of peace will be with you"* (v. 9). Everything you learned and received from me, do those things. We can see that Paul's doctrine and life were the same. What they saw in him was the same thing they heard from him. He could show his life as well as his doctrine as an example for them to follow. It is incredibly effective and powerful when we can say things to others and it is the same as what they have seen in us. And this is the way to have the God of peace with us—to keep close to our duty to him. The Lord is with us while we are with him.

Daily Reflection

Paul wrote about two-thirds of the New Testament. Most of our directives about being Christians come from his letters to the different churches. They are filled with instructions on almost every conceivable aspect of a life of faith. It is no surprise that he speaks often about prayer. It's also no surprise that he speaks often about himself praying for others and needing prayer himself. He realized what an important part of his spiritual walk it was to pray.

1. What is the significance of asking to be of one mind with other Christians?
2. Why do you think Paul repeats himself in his encouragement to rejoice in the Lord?
3. Do you think it's possible to live a life without worrying? What is the cure?
4. What does it mean to be in constant prayer?
5. How do we get the peace that passes understanding? Have you ever felt this?

16

THE PRAYER OF A RIGHTEOUS PERSON

The prayer of a righteous person has great power as it is working.
James 5:16

The great advantage and power of prayer are shown and proved: *"The prayer of a righteous person has great power as it is working,"* whether he prays for himself or others.

He who prays must be a righteous person, not in an absolute sense but in a gospel sense—not loving or approving any sin. *"If I had cherished iniquity in my heart, the Lord would not have listened"* (Psalm 66:18). Also, the prayer itself must be a passionate prayer. It must be a pouring out of the heart to God, and it must come from genuine faith. This kind of prayer has great power. It is an advantage to ourselves, it might be very beneficial to our friends, and we are assured it is acceptable to God.

The power of prayer is shown in the success of Elijah. This can encourage us in common circumstances if we see that Elijah was a man like us. He was a devoted and great man, but he had his weaknesses and was subject to temptation as well as others. In prayer, we must not look at the merit of the person, but to the grace of God. This is how we should copy Elijah—that he prayed sincerely. It is not enough to say a prayer, but we must pray in prayer. Our thoughts must be focused, our desires firm and passionate, and our attitudes in check. Then, when we pray in prayer, we pray effectively.

Elijah went off to pray because even though God had promised rain, he had to ask for it: *"Ask rain from the LORD in the season of the spring rain, from the Lord who makes the storm clouds, and he will give them showers of rain"* (Zech. 10:1). He also went off alone to give thanks for God's answer of sending down fire, now hoping for an answer of water. What he said, we do not know, but we do see:

He went to a strange place. Elijah traveled alone to the top of Mount Carmel, which was very high and very private, and which we read about in Amos 9:3. There he wanted to be alone. Those who are called to appear and act in public for God must still find time to be alone with him and continue praying in private. There Elijah set himself on his watchtower as in Habakkuk 2:1.

He prayed in a strange posture. He fell down on his knees, in a sign of humility, reverence, and urgency, and put his face between his knees (he bowed his head so low that it touched his knees), humbling himself now that God had honored him.

Then Elijah ordered his servant to tell him as soon as he saw a cloud appearing from the Mediterranean Sea, which was very visible from the top of Carmel. Six times his servant goes to the top of the hill and sees nothing, bringing no good news to his master. Still, Elijah continues praying; he will not be distracted even to go and see with his own eyes but sends his servant to see if there is a cloud. Elijah keeps his mind focused and intent in prayer, and stays in that attitude, as a person who has taken up Jacob's resolution: *"I will not let you go unless you bless me"* (Gen. 32:26). Even though the answer of our passionate and believing supplications does not come quickly, we must continue in prayer and not lose heart or draw back, because, in the end, it will speak and not lie.

Elijah prayed that it would not rain, and God heard him pleading against an idolatrous persecuting country so that it did not rain for three years and six months. Again he prayed, and it rained. So, we see prayer is the key that opens and closes heaven. This example of the extraordinary power of prayer is to encourage ordinary Christians to be sincere in prayer. If Elijah, by prayer, could do such great and wonderful things, surely the prayers of a righteous person shall not return empty. There may not be as many miracles in God's answering our prayers, but there will be much grace.

Daily Reflection

One of the ways to learn about how to live as a Christian is to look at the examples of those who have walked before us. We have so many of these in the Bible; their accounts are recorded, not just for the sake of stories but for modeling our lives on the way they behaved in situations. Elijah often seems way out of reach, a man who lived large and did things we will never do. But we are told he was a man just like us, and his prayers brought about incredible miracles.

1. What is your picture of Elijah? Do you think he was a person like us?
2. Read James 5:17 to substantiate your answer to the first question.
3. Do you ever pray passionately, pouring out your heart? Or do you hold back with quiet, dead words?
4. What do we learn about the place and posture of Elijah's prayer?
5. What makes a righteous person's prayers effective and powerful?

17

PRAYING FOR OTHERS

And the prayer of faith will save the one who is sick.
James 5:15

Verse 13 says, *"Is anyone among you suffering? Let him pray. Is anyone cheerful? Let him sing praise."* This tells us to pray for ourselves. Verse 14 says, *"Is anyone among you sick? Let him call for the elders of the church, and let them pray over him."* This tells us to ask for the prayers of ministers. And verse 16, *"Confess your sins to one another and pray for one another,"* tells us Christians to pray one for another. So, we have three types of prayer recommended: ministerial, social, and secret.

Praying for the Sick

We have been given specific directions when praying for the sick. They must:

Go to the elders of the church (v. 14-15). It is the sick people's duty to send for ministers and to want their help and prayers.

It is the duty of ministers to pray over the sick when called for. Let them pray, let their prayers be suited to the case.

In times of miraculous healing, the sick must be anointed with oil in the name of the Lord. In Mark 6:13, we read the apostle was anointing many who were sick with oil, and healing them. Some argue that it was only for a special time or certain people, and the use of anointing with oil has been misused. However, there is one thing to be seen here: The saving of the sick is not due to the anointing with oil but to prayer. *"And the prayer of faith will save the one who is sick."*

Prayer for the sick must come from, and be accompanied by, faith. There must be faith in the person praying and in the person being prayed for. In a time of sickness, it is not the cold and formal prayer that is powerful, but the prayer of faith.

We can see the success of prayer. *"The Lord will raise him up."* That is, if God has planned for that person to do more in the world. And, if they have committed sins, these will be forgiven—where sickness is sent as a punishment for some specific sin, that sin will be forgiven, and the sickness will be removed. Just as Jesus said to the lame man, *"Sin no more, that nothing worse may happen to you"* (John 5:14), it is seen that some specific sin was the cause of his sickness. So, the main thing we should beg God for ourselves and others in sickness is the forgiveness of sin. Sin is the root of sickness and the sting of it. If sin is forgiven, either affliction will be removed or we will see there is mercy in it carrying on. When healing is based on forgiveness, we can say as Hezekiah did: *"In love you have delivered my life from the pit of destruction"* (Isa. 38:17). When you are sick and in pain, it is common to pray and cry, "Give me relief! Restore me to health!" But your prayer should rather be "God forgive my sins!"

Confessing to Others

Christians are told to confess their faults to each other, and to join together: *"Therefore, confess your sins to one another and pray for one another, that you may be healed."* Some connect this verse with verse 14; when sick people ask ministers to pray over them, they should also confess their sins to them. Anyone who knows their sickness is a punishment for some specific sin, and they cannot ask for healing without first asking God for the forgiveness of that sin, should confess it to the pastor so he knows how to pray correctly for them.

But the confession in this verse is for one Christian to another, and not to a priest. Where people have hurt one another, injustice must be confessed to those against whom they have been done. Where people have tempted one another to sin or have been involved in the same evil deeds, they should encourage each other to repent. Where wrongs are publicly known, these should be publicly confessed, so everyone concerned knows. And sometimes it is good to confess our faults to a minister or praying friend, as they can help us to beg God for mercy and forgiveness.

But James is not telling us to share everything we know is wrong in ourselves or each other. Confession is necessary for our reconciliation with those we have wronged, or for understanding the situation so we can confess our faults. And sometimes it is also good for Christians to reveal their weaknesses to each other if there is a strong friendship and relationship, so they can help each other through their prayers to find forgiveness for their sins. Those who confess their faults to each other should pray with and for one another.

Daily Reflection

We are not only supposed to pray for our own needs and desires but to pray for others as well. Sometimes that means praying for those who are sick or not well in their spirits. Henry sticks closely to the verses without adding too much of his own opinions, letting the Bible speak for itself. It is clear that, whoever we pray for and however we pray for them, faith is a key element here.

1. Have you ever prayed for someone who was sick? What happened?
2. Why do you think sin and sickness are so closely linked?
3. What is the power of confession? Read 1 John 1:9.
4. Why is faith so important when it comes to praying for others to be healed?

18

A PRAYER OF REPENTANCE

Create in me a clean heart, O God,
and renew a right spirit within me.
Cast me not away from your presence,
and take not your Holy Spirit from me.
Restore to me the joy of your salvation,
and uphold me with a willing spirit.
Psalm 51:10-12

This is David's most well-known psalm of repentance. David prays that God would wash his sins away. *"Purge me with hyssop"* (v. 7). The expression is a ceremonial cleansing of lepers or unclean people with a bunch of hyssop. But it also speaks of gospel-grace: Purge me with the blood of Jesus applied to my soul. It is the blood of Jesus (called the blood of sprinkling, Heb. 12:24) that purges the conscience from dead works, from that guilt of sin and fear of God that breaks our communion with him. If Jesus' blood cleanses us from our sin, then we shall be truly clean (Heb. 10:2). If we are washed in this fountain, we will be whiter than snow, not only acquitted but accepted. *"Though your sins are like scarlet, they shall be as white as snow"* (Isa. 1:18).

Now his sin is forgiven, he prays that he might have the comfort of that forgiveness. *"Let me hear joy and gladness; let the bones that you have broken rejoice"* (v. 8). He prays to have solid peace. The pain of a heart broken for sin is compared to a broken bone. The comfort and joy that come from forgiveness to a penitent sinner are as refreshing as being released from the worst pain. David desires that God would look on him and put joy into his heart, that he would be reconciled to him, which is a further act of grace.

He prays for complete forgiveness. *"Hide your face from my sins"* (v. 9). Do not be provoked by them to deal with me as I deserve. My sins are always before me, let them be thrown away behind your back. *"Blot out all my iniquities"* (v. 9). Delete them, as a cloud is wiped out by the rays of the sun (Isa. 44:22).

He prays for sanctifying grace. He does not pray, "Lord, preserve my reputation," as Saul did. David's main concern is to have his corrupt nature changed. He prays, *"Create in me a clean heart, O God"* (v. 10). He saw what an unclean heart he had, and that he has no power to fix it, and begs of God to create a clean heart in him. Only God who made the heart can make it new again. He created the world by his word, and it is by his word that we are clean (John 15:3), that we are sanctified (John 17:17). He saw the chaos the sin had brought and so he prays, *"And renew a right spirit within me"* (v. 10). Lord, repair the spiritual damage this sin has caused and put me right again. Renew a constant spirit in me, not the inconstancy and inconsistency he had experienced in sin.

He prays for God's goodwill toward him and his good work in him. *"Cast me not away from your presence"* (v. 11). David prays that he might not be thrown out of God's protection, but that he might be under his guiding wisdom and in his caring power, and not be forbidden communion with God. He also prays that he might never be deprived of God's grace. *"Take not your Holy Spirit from me"* (v. 11). He knew he had grieved the Spirit and caused him to withdraw. We are lost if God takes his Holy Spirit from us. Saul was a sad example of this. David knew this and begs, "Lord, whatever you take from me—my children, my crown, my life—do not take not your Holy Spirit from me" (2 Sam. 7:15).

He prays for spiritual advantages and grace. David finds two effects of his sin: It made him sad, and so he prays, *"Restore to me the joy of your salvation"* (v. 12). A Christian knows no better joy than the joy of God's salvation, in his Savior, and in eternal life. When we doubt our salvation, how can we expect the joy of it? But, when we repent, we can pray and hope that God will restore that joy to us. David also saw that it made him weak, and so he prays, *"Uphold me with a willing spirit"* (v. 12). He knew he had behaved deceitfully, his behavior was terrible. "Lord," he says, "let your Spirit inspire my soul with noble and generous principles, that I may always behave in that way." A free, willing spirit will be a firm and solid spirit.

Daily Reflection

Repentance is not a once-off event that we go through when we are born again. It is to be done daily. It brings us into a humble, contrite, and broken state before God so He can lift us up again to have a perfect, unblemished relationship with Him. David understood this more than anyone else. It's why this psalm speaks so powerfully as a prayer of repentance. Looking at what he understood, realized, and brought before the Lord, we can learn what it is to have a penitent heart in prayer.

1. Do you bring your sin before God on a regular basis, asking for forgiveness?
2. What does it mean to repent?
3. The word purge is used specifically here. Why is it such a powerful, effective way of asking God to take our sins away?
4. Why was David so concerned with not being in God's presence or having the Holy Spirit?
5. What do you think the "joy of my salvation" means?

19

PRAYER IS ARMOR

*"Praying at all times in the Spirit, with all prayer and supplication.
To that end, keep alert with all perseverance,
making supplication for all the saints"*
Ephesians 6:18

Paul encourages us in our Christian warfare. Is life not warfare? It is because we struggle with the common trials of human life. Is our faith not more of a warfare? It is because we struggle against the powers of darkness, and with many enemies who want to keep us from God and heaven. We have enemies to fight against, a captain to fight for, a flag to fight under, and certain rules of war that govern us. *"Finally, be strong in the Lord and in the strength of his might"* (Eph. 6:10). It is essential that a soldier is courageous and well-armed.

If Christians are soldiers of Jesus, they must be well-armed: *"Put on the whole armor of God, that you may be able to stand against the schemes of the devil"* (Eph. 6:11). Make use of all the proper defenses and weapons for fighting off the temptations and strategies of Satan—get and exercise all the Christian qualities, the whole armor, that no part is exposed to the enemy.

It is called the armor of God because he prepares and gives it. We have no armor of our own that will stand up in times of trial. Nothing is good enough but the armor of God. This armor is prepared for us, but we must put it on—we must pray for grace, we must use the grace given to us, and use it when necessary. The reason we should be completely armed is that we will be able to stand against the tricks of the devil —that we can hold out and overcome all the deception, snares, and schemes he brings against us.

Prayer must buckle on all the other parts of our Christian armor. *"Praying at all times in the Spirit, with all prayer and supplication."* We must join prayer with all these qualities, for our defense against these spiritual enemies, asking God for help and assistance when we need it. We must always pray. We do not do anything else but pray because there are other duties of faith that must be done. But, we should be constantly in a time of prayer. We must pray on all occasions, and as often as our own and others' needs call us to it. We must always be in an attitude of prayer and should mix spontaneous prayers with other duties, and with our daily work. Even though set times and personal prayer cannot always happen—when other duties are to be done—holy spontaneous expressions can.

We must pray with all prayer and supplication, with all kinds of prayer: public, private and secret, social and solitary, solemn and sudden. We must pray with all the parts of prayer: confession of sin, request for mercy, and thanksgivings for blessings received. We must pray in the Spirit; our spirits must be linked in the duty and we must do it by the grace of God's Spirit. We must do our best to keep our hearts in a praying attitude, in every situation, taking every opportunity to do so. We must focus every emotion of our own hearts toward the duty.

When God says, *"Seek my face,"* our hearts must obey (Psalm 27:8). This we must do with all perseverance. We must continue in prayer, whatever happens in our physical circumstances, and we must continue praying as long as we live in the world. We must persevere in prayer, not cutting it short —when our hearts are keen and there is time for it. We must also persevere in specific requests, no matter what discouragements come our way. And we must pray with supplication; not for ourselves only, but for all Christians, because we are members one of another.

Daily Reflection

Ephesians 6 is commonly known as the portion of the Bible that teaches us about the armor of God. It lists many of the spiritual aspects like faith, salvation, and righteousness. But prayer is often left off because it is not distinctly linked as a part of the armor. And yet, it is a vital piece of weaponry we need in order to withstand the attacks of Satan.

1. Do you experience Christian life as a type of warfare? How?
2. What does it mean to be a soldier of Jesus? See 2 Timothy 2:1.
3. Look in Ephesians 6. How many times does it say fight? How many times does it say we must stand? What is the difference?
4. What does Henry mean by saying God prepares and gives us the armor?
5. What does it mean to keep our hearts in a praying attitude?

20

THE ORDER OF PRAYER

"Lord, teach us to pray"
Luke 11:1

Even though I recommend a good method for prayer here, and that which has been generally approved, I am far from thinking we should always tie ourselves to it. We can change it as much as we can change the words: Thanksgiving can sometimes be put before confession or petition, or our intercessions for others before our petitions for ourselves, as in the Lord's prayer. Sometimes one of these parts of prayer may be enlarged much more than another, or they may be decently interwoven in some other method.

Adoration

This is the first part of prayer, which is an address to God and adoration of him, with proper acknowledgments, professions, and preparatory requests.

We must come with reverent and serious spirits, our thoughts not wandering, and everything in us focused on God so we can perform the duty that lies before us. With an active faith, we must set the Lord before us, see that he is watching us, and come into his special presence, presenting ourselves to him as living sacrifices, which we want to be holy and acceptable, and a reasonable service to him (Rom. 12:1). Then we must tie these sacrifices to the horns of the altar (Psalm 118:27).

Confession

The second part of prayer is the confession of sin, complaints of ourselves, and humble declarations of repentance.

Having given glory to God, which is due to him, we must humble ourselves before Him in the sense of our own sinfulness and wickedness. In that state, we must give glory to him, as our judge, by whom we deserve to be condemned, and yet hope, through Christ, to be acquitted and set free. *"Give glory to the Lord God of Israel and give praise to him. And tell me now what you have done; do not hide it from me"* (Josh. 7:19).

Petitions and Requests

The third part of prayer is petition and supplication for the good things which we need.

Having opened the wounds of sin, its guilt and power still in us, we must next seek God for the remedy, for healing and help. It can only be expected from him, and that is why we ask him. And now we must realize how much we need those mercies that we pray for, that we are forever lost without them. Seeing their incredible value, we are happy if we receive them. We must be like Jacob wrestling with him in prayer as if it was for our lives and the lives of our souls. But we must not think in our prayers to prescribe to him, or in persistence to persuade him. He knows us better than we know ourselves, and knows what he will do (John 6:6). But, we reveal our needs and our desires, and then bring ourselves to his wisdom and goodness. We give honor to Him as our protector and provider, and by faith plead his promise with him. If we are sincere in this, we are qualified through his grace in the new covenant to receive His blessings, and can be confident that we do and will receive them (Mark 11:24).

Thanksgivings for Mercy

The fourth part of prayer is thanksgiving for the mercies we have received from God, and the many blessings we hope to benefit from.

Our job at the throne of grace is not only to find favor with God but to give him the glory due to his name, not only in adoration of his characteristics but a grateful acknowledgment of his goodness to us. This thanksgiving cannot add anything to His glory, but He is pleased to accept it and be glorified by it. As long as it comes from a humble heart that's aware of its own unworthiness to receive any favor from God, that values the gifts and loves the one who gives them.

Intercede for Others

The fifth part of prayer is intercession or supplication to God for others.

Jesus taught us to pray, not only with but for others. Paul said we must make supplication for all Christians—many of his prayers in his letters are for his friends. We must not think that when we are praying for them that we are not passionate, and mediocre about it, because it does not personally concern us, but we must have a holy fire of love both to God and man to make our devotions even more motivated (Eph. 6:18).

Intercede for Specifics

This part consists of addressing God about specific personal or general issues that come up.

It is our duty, and cure against worry, that in everything by prayer and supplication with thanksgiving we make our requests known to God (Phil. 4:6). Here, we have confidence and freedom to state our case, and seek to him for relief (Heb. 10:19). Not that God needs to be informed specifically of our condition because he knows it better than we do ourselves. It is his will that we acknowledge him in all our ways (Prov. 3:6), and wait on him for the direction of every step (Psalm 37:23), not prescribing but subscribing to infinite wisdom, humbly showing him our needs, burdens, and desires, and then bringing ourselves to him, to do what he thinks is best.

Conclusion

This is when we end our prayers.

We are commanded to always pray, to pray without ceasing, and to continue in prayer, because we must always have a tendency toward doing it, be constant in it, and never grow tired of it, or give it up. But, we cannot always be praying, we must come down from this mountain. We cannot continue too long, or it becomes extra work for us or those that join us. We have other work we have to do. Jacob wrestles with the angel, but he must go because the morning is coming. Therefore, we must think of concluding. The prayers of David have to end. We must conclude, but also keep the thought of prayer in our hearts.

Daily Reflection

This is taken from Henry's *A Method for Prayer* book which expands this idea of having an order and provides biblical words for each of the parts. It is a very helpful tool to read through and use for those of us who are learning how to pray. Henry admits that we do not always have to stick to the order he prescribes, but he gives it to us as a helpful guide to keep us from getting lost in our own thoughts and words.

1. Have a look at the order of prayer. Do you ever pray in this order?
2. Do you think this format is beneficial to prayer or not?
3. Why do you think confession comes so soon in prayer?
4. Do you think it's possible to use an order like this but still have the freedom to express ourselves?

21

PERSISTENT WIDOW

They ought always to pray and not lose heart.
Luke 18:1

Jesus told this parable to teach us that people *"ought always to pray and not lose heart."* It assumes that all Christians are praying people, all Christians have a constant and occasional correspondence with him; they pray every day, and in every emergency. It is our privilege and honor to pray. It is our duty. We ought to pray, we sin if we neglect it. It should be our constant work. We ought always to pray, it is a duty we must fulfill every day. We must pray, and never grow tired of praying, nor give it up until we get to heaven.

Jesus shows the power of persistence among people who will be persuaded to do what is right when nothing else will influence them. He gives us an example of an honest cause that succeeded with an unjust judge, not because it was fair and right but purely because of persistence.

What the parable does is teach us constancy and perseverance in our requests for some spiritual blessings we are looking for, either for ourselves or the church. When we are praying for strength against our spiritual enemies, our lusts and corruptions, which are our worst enemies, we must continue in prayer; we must pray and not lose heart because we do not seek God's face in vain. Jesus told this parable to encourage Christians to pray with faith and passion and to persevere in it.

He assures us that in time, God will be gracious to us. *"Will not God give justice to his elect, who cry to him day and night?"* (Luke 18:7).

What is it that we desire and expect? That God would give us justice.

There are those who are God's people, his elect, his chosen people. He watches over them in all he does for them. It is because they are his chosen.

God's chosen people meet with lots of trouble and opposition in this world. There are many enemies that fight against them, Satan being their greatest.

What we want and wait for is God's preserving and protecting us, his work in us, his securing the interest of the church in the world, and his grace in the heart.

What must we do to get this? We must cry day and night to him, not that he needs our complaints, or is persuaded by our begging, but he has made it our duty, and if we do it, he has promised mercy. We should be specific when praying against our spiritual enemies, as Paul was: *"I pleaded with the Lord about this, that it should leave me"* (2 Cor. 12:8), like this persistent widow. "Lord, strengthen me against this temptation." We must wrestle with God, as people who know how to value the blessing, and will not be told, "No!" God's praying people are told to give him no rest (Isa. 62:6-7).

What discouragements can we expect in our prayers? He might wait and not come immediately in answer to our prayers. He shows patience toward our enemies and does not take vengeance on them. He shows us patience and does not plead for us.

Assurances We Have of Being Heard

What assurance do we have that those blessings will come, even though they are delayed?

This widow was a stranger to the judge, but God's praying people are his own elect, whom he knows, loves, delights in, and is always concerned about.

She was only one, but the praying people of God are many, all of whom come to him on the same errand, and agree to ask what they need (Matt. 18:19). As the saints of heaven surround the throne of glory with their united praises, so saints on earth besiege the throne of grace with their united prayers.

She came to a judge who told her to stay away. We come to a Father that tells us to come boldly to him, and teaches us to cry, "Abba, Father."

She came to an unjust judge. We come to a righteous Father (John 17:25) who regards his own glory and the comforts of his children, especially those in need, like widows and orphans.

She came to this judge on her own account. God is engaged in the cause which we are asking for, and we can say, *"Arise, O God, defend your cause" "What will you do for your great name?"* (Psalm 74:22, Josh. 7:9).

She had no friend to speak for her, to add weight to her request. We have an advocate with the Father, his own Son, who lives to make intercession for us and has a powerful interest in heaven.

She had no promise given to her or any encouragement to ask. We are told to ask with a promise that it will be given to us.

She could only get to the judge at certain times. We can cry to God day and night, at all hours, and have a hope that we will succeed through persistence.

Her persistence provoked the judge and could have irritated him more against her. Our persistence is pleasing to God. The prayer of the righteous is his delight, and therefore, we can hope we will succeed if it is an effective, passionate prayer.

The success she had was her continually harassing the judge: *"Because this widow keeps bothering me, I will give her justice, so that she will not beat me down by her continual coming"* (Luke 18:5). So, she gained justice by continual asking; she begged it at his door, followed him in the streets, solicited him in court, and still her cry was, *"Give me justice against my adversary"* (Luke 18:3), which he was forced to do, to get rid of her.

Daily Reflection

Jesus' parable of the persistent widow and the unjust judge is a key for us to become effective people who pray. Persistence and perseverance are important aspects when it comes to powerful prayer, and there are many examples of strong Christians who were always on their knees before God, bringing the same requests again and again until they were answered. In this world of instant gratification, we have lost some of that determination to push on until we have our reply.

1. Henry says it is a privilege to pray. Do you feel this in your prayer times?
2. Are you able to pray for something without giving up?
3. Why do you think God requires us to persevere in prayer?
4. Why is it important to be assured the answer will come, even if it is delayed?

22

USING ARGUMENTS IN PRAYER

I would lay my case before him
and fill my mouth with arguments.
Job 23:4

In Exodus 32, Moses intercedes with God on behalf of Israel. We should have the same attitude when we come to the throne of grace for the church and our friends. Here, Moses is standing in the gap to turn away the judgment of God. *"Therefore he said he would destroy them—had not Moses, his chosen one, stood in the breach before him, to turn away his wrath from destroying them"* (Psalm 106:23). He wisely took the hint God gave him when he said, *"Let me alone"* (v. 10), which, though it seemed to forbid his interceding, actually encouraged it by showing what power the prayer of faith has with God.

Let us look at Moses' prayer: He tells God, *"Turn from your burning anger"* (v. 12). It is not as if he thought God had no right to be angry, but he begs that he would not be so angry as to destroy Israel. "Let mercy rejoice against judgment; repent of this evil; change the sentence of destruction into one of correction." He turns to his pleas, and he fills his mouth with arguments, not to move God but to express his own faith and to motivate his own passion in prayer.

He urges God's interest in them, the great things he had already done for them, and the many blessings and miracles he had performed for them (v. 11). God had said to Moses, they are *"your people, whom you brought up out of the land of Egypt"* (v. 7), but Moses humbly turns this back on God again: "They are your people, you are their Lord and owner. I am just their servant. You brought them out of Egypt, I was only the instrument in your hand. That was done for their deliverance which only you could do." Even though he should be angry with them for setting up another god, it was still a reason why he should not be so angry with them as to destroy them. Nothing is more natural than for a father to correct his son, but nothing is more unnatural than for a father to kill his son.

And as the relationship is a good plea—"They are *your people*" (v. 11)—so is the experience they had had of his kindness to them: "You brought them out of Egypt, though they were unworthy, and had served the gods of the Egyptians (Josh. 24:15). If you did that for them, despite their sins in Egypt, will you undo it because of their sins in the wilderness?"

He pleads the concern of God's glory. *"Why should the Egyptians say, 'With evil intent did he bring them out, to kill them'"* (v. 12). Israel is like a family to Moses, like his children, but it is the glory of God that he is most concerned about. This is closer to his heart than anything else. If Israel died without any disgrace to God's name, Moses would be happy to sit down contented, but he cannot bear to hear God seen in a bad light, so he asks the question, "What will the Egyptians say?" Their eyes, and the eyes of all the neighboring nations, were now on Israel. From the miraculous beginnings of that people, they had high expectations of something great happening in the end. But, if these people who were so incredibly saved should be suddenly ruined, what would the world say of it, especially the Egyptians, who had such a hatred for Israel and the God of Israel? They would say, "God was either weak and could not, or he was fickle and would not, complete the salvation he began. He brought them to that mountain, not to sacrifice but to be sacrificed." They will not consider how Israel had provoked their own God to justify the judgment but will think it was because God and his people could not agree. They will think that the Israelites' God had done that which the Egyptians wanted to be done and so it was their victory, not Israel's.

The glorifying of God's name should be our first petition; as it is in the Lord's Prayer, so it should also be our greatest plea (Psalm 79:9). *"Do not dishonor your glorious throne"* (Jer. 14:21). And if we want to plead this with God as a reason why he should not destroy us, we should plead it with ourselves as a reason why we should not offend him: "What will the Egyptians say?" We should always be careful that the name of God and his doctrine are not blasphemed through us.

He pleads God's promise to the patriarchs: *"Remember Abraham, Isaac, and Israel,"* that he would multiply their seed, and give them the land of Canaan for an inheritance—a promise confirmed by an oath, an oath by himself, since he could swear by no greater (v. 13). God's promises are to be our arguments in prayer, because what he has promised, he is able to perform, and the honor of this truth is in it being done. "Lord, if Israel is cut off, what will become of the promise? Shall their unbelief cause that to be ineffectual? God forbid it." So, we must take our encouragement in prayer only from God.

Daily Reflection

At first, it may seem odd that we are told to use arguments in our prayers for them to be more effective. Is it right to argue with God? But, this is not when we have a disagreement or a quarrel, it's to back up our requests and state our case properly. Many of the great men of God used this method of praying when they wanted to prove to God that what they were asking of him was right and in his will. We can use the same techniques in our own prayers.

1. Have you ever used arguments to back up your prayers with God?
2. Why do you think it makes them more effective?
3. How do we use God's promises as our arguments?

4. What is the difference between demanding of the Lord and asking confidently?

23

THE PHARISEE'S PRAYER

The Pharisee, standing by himself, prayed thus:
"God, I thank you that I am not like other men"
Luke 18:11

Here is the Pharisee's address to God (I cannot call it a prayer). *"The Pharisee, standing by himself, prayed."* This means he was either completely focused on himself, could see nothing but self, his own praise, and not God's glory; or he was standing in some place everyone could see, where he distinguished himself; or he set himself up with lots of status and formality. All this shows:

His Arrogance

That he trusted he was righteous. He said many good things about himself, which might all be true. He had no scandalous sins, he was not a blackmailer, not a loan shark, not oppressive to debtors or tenants, but fair and kind to everyone. He was not unfair, he wronged no one, and like Samuel, he could say, *Whose ox have I taken? Or whose donkey have I taken?* (1 Sam. 12:3). He was not an adulterer, but kept his body holy. This was not all. He fasted twice a week, partly out of show, partly of devotion. The Pharisees and their disciples fasted twice a week, Monday and Thursday. So, he glorified God with his body. But, that was not all. He gave tithes of everything he had, according to the law, and so glorified God with wealth.

Now, this is all very good and commendable. What a pity for anyone who does not match up to the righteousness of this Pharisee, and yet he was not accepted. Why not?

Giving God thanks for this, even though it is good, seems to only be a formality. He does not say, *"But by the grace of God I am what I am"* (1 Cor. 15:10), as Paul did, but dismisses it with an insult, *"God, I thank you,"* which is used as a plausible introduction to a proud self-indulgent show of himself.

He boasts about this and dwells on this subject as if his whole reason for coming to the temple was to tell God Almighty how good he was. He is ready to say, along with those hypocrites we read of in Isaiah 58:3, *"Why have we fasted, and you see it not?"*

He trusted it as a righteousness, and not only mentioned it but pleaded it, as if this was deserved from God, and put him in his debt.

There is not one word of real prayer in everything he says. He went up to the temple to pray, but forgot what he was supposed to do, was so full of himself and his own goodness that he thought he lacked nothing—not even the favor and grace of God, which he did not seem to think about asking for.

His Pride

That he despised others.

He thought badly of everyone but himself: *"I thank you that I am not like other men."* He speaks as if he was better than everyone. We might have a reason to thank God that we are not like some people who are notoriously wicked and evil but to speak generally, as if we are the only one who is good, and everyone else is a villain, is to judge indiscriminately.

He specifically thought badly of the tax collector, whom he had left behind, with the Gentiles in the outer court. He knew that he was a tax collector, and therefore, concluded that he was an extortioner, unjust, and everything else that is bad. Maybe it was true, and he knew about it, but what business was that of his? Could he not say his prayers without scolding those around him? Or was this a part of his *"God, I thank you"*? Was he as pleased with the tax collector's badness as he was with his own goodness? There could not be better proof, not only of the lack of humility and love but of reigning pride and hatred, than this prayer.

The proud Pharisee goes away, rejected by God. His prayer is so far from being accepted that it is an insult. He is not justified, his sins are not forgiven, nor is he delivered from condemnation. He is not accepted as righteous in God's sight, because he is so righteous in his own sight.

Daily Reflection

Have your Bible close by as you work through all of these readings and daily reflections. Henry uses a lot of scripture, and it is helpful to look them up as you go along. If there are any verses that link to these, look them up as well. Studying the word is important if we want to learn anything about God and about praying. Write the verses down. Learn them if you can. It's important to always look back at what the Bible says about something. It should be our ultimate guide and plumbline in everything.

1. After reading this, what is your personal view of the Pharisee? Do you know anyone like this? Are you like this in any way?
2. If some of his words were correct, what made them an insult before God?
3. Read James 4:6. How does this tie in with the parable of the Pharisee and tax collector?
4. Why is pride such a dangerous thing in prayer?
5. Why do you think God hates hypocrites so much?

24

THE TAX COLLECTOR'S PRAYER

But the tax collector, standing far off,
would not even lift up his eyes to heaven,
but beat his breast, saying,
"God, be merciful to me, a sinner!"
Luke 18:13

Here is the tax collector's address to God, which was the opposite of the Pharisee's—as full of humility and humiliation as his was of pride and show; as full of repentance for sin, and desire toward God, as his was of confidence in himself and his own righteousness and sufficiency.

His Attitude

He expressed his repentance and humility in what he did. His gesture, when he prayed, was full of sincerity and humility—the proper clothing of a broken, repentant, and obedient heart.

He was *"standing far off."* The Pharisee stood, but as high as he could at the upper end of the court where it was crowded. The tax collector kept at a distance, sensing his unworthiness to draw near to God, and perhaps out of fear of offending the Pharisee, whom he noticed looked down on him, and of disturbing his devotions. He knew that God might only want to see him from far off and send him away from him eternally and that it was a great favor that God would admit him that close.

He *"would not even lift up his eyes to heaven,"* or his hands, which was normal in prayer. He did lift up his heart to God, in holy desires, but through his shame and humiliation, he did not lift up his eyes in holy confidence and courage. He was drowning in his sin like a heavy burden so that he was not able to look up: *"My iniquities have overtaken me, and I cannot see"* (Psalm 40:12). This is an indication of the dejection of his mind at the thought of sin.

He *"beat his breast"* in a holy dissatisfaction with his sin: "I would beat this wicked heart of mine, the poisoned fountain out of which flows all the streams of sin if I could get to it." The sinner's heart first chastises him in a repentant rebuke (2 Sam. 24:10). David's heart chastised him. Sinner, what have you done? And then he beats his heart in repentant regret: *"Wretched man that I am!"* (Rom. 7:24). Great mourners are shown beating on their breasts (Nah. 2:7).

His Words

He expressed it in what he said. His prayer was short. Fear and shame stopped him from saying too much. Sighs and groans swallowed up his words, but what he said was enough: *"God, be merciful to me, a sinner!"* What a blessing for us to have this prayer on record as an answered prayer, and that we are sure that the person who prayed it went home justified. We will also be justified if we pray it like he did, through Jesus. "God, be merciful to me, a sinner. May the God of infinite mercy be merciful to me, because if you do not, I will be lost forever, forever miserable. God, be merciful to me, for I have been cruel to myself."

He admits he is a sinner by nature, by practice, guilty before God. Look, I am evil, what more can I say? The Pharisee denies that he is a sinner, none of his neighbors can accuse him, and he sees no reason to accuse himself of anything—he is clean, and he is pure from sin. But the tax collector says he is nothing else but a sinner, a convicted criminal before God.

He depends on nothing except the mercy of God—that is all he relies on. The Pharisee insisted on the merit of his fasting and tithes, but the poor tax collector does not think of merit, runs to mercy as a refugee, and takes hold of the horn of that altar. "Justice condemns me, nothing will save me but mercy."

He prays sincerely for the benefit of that mercy: "God, be merciful, show favor to me. Forgive my sins, be reconciled to me, take me into your favor, receive me graciously, and love me freely." He comes like a beggar for coins when he is ready to die from hunger. He probably repeated this prayer with renewed emotions, and perhaps said more along the same lines, made a specific confession of his sins, and mentioned the mercies he wanted, and waited on God for. But, the burden of his song was still, *"God, be merciful to me, a sinner!"*

The tax collector, on this humble address to heaven, gains forgiveness of his sins. The one whom the Pharisee would not count worthy of his own dog's company, God counts as worthy to be included with the children of his family. The reason for this is that God's glory resists the proud and gives grace to the humble.

Daily Reflection

Jesus' use of parables in teaching people was clever because it gave us real-life examples of spiritual things that are not easily seen or understood. This second part of the parable from Luke 18 is the complete opposite of the Pharisee. Jesus specifically chose two characters to bring his message of prayer across to those who were listening. For us, Henry takes it even further by looking at each aspect of how they entered, stood, and what they said. It is important for us to see these in our own lives as well, so it does not just stay as a story, but a life application.

1. Why did Jesus choose to use a tax collector as his second example?
2. What are the ways the tax collector is different from the Pharisee?

3. Have you ever come before God in the same way as the tax collector did, unable to look at God?
4. Why is praying for mercy such an important part of this prayer?
5. Look again at James 4:6, and at your own life now that you have read both parts of the parable. Which one are you?

25

DAVID'S PRAYER

O LORD, I call upon you; hasten to me!
Give ear to my voice when I call to you!
Psalm 141:1-4

We are taught to ask two things from David's prayer: mercy to accept what we do well, and grace to keep us from doing wrong.

A Prayer to Be Heard

David loved prayer, and he begs God to hear and answer his prayers. David cried to God. His crying shows the passion in his prayer; he prayed as someone sincere. His crying to God shows faith and focus in prayer. And what did he want from his prayer?

That God would be aware of it: *"Give ear to my voice when I call to you!"* Those who cry in prayer can hope to be heard in prayer, not because they are loud, but their enthusiasm.

That he would come to him: *"Hasten to me!"* Those who know how to value God's presence will push for it. The person who prays will be keen for God to come quickly.

That God would be pleased with him in it: *"Let my prayer be counted as incense before you, and the lifting up of my hands as the evening sacrifice!"* (v. 2). He wants God to be pleased with his praying and lifting hands in prayer, which shows the elevation and enlargement of his desire and the expression of his hope and expectation. Lifting hands signifies lifting up the heart, instead of lifting up the sacrifices which were heaved and waved before the Lord. Prayer is a spiritual sacrifice—it is the offering up of the soul to God.

Now, he prays that this will come before God like the burnt on the golden altar and the evening sacrifice. Those that pray in faith can expect it will please God better than an animal sacrifice. David could not attend the sacrifice and incense and begged that his prayer might be received instead. Prayer is a sweet-smelling aroma to God, but just as incense has no smell without fire, prayer must have the fire of holy love and passion.

A Prayer to Be Kept

David was wary of sin, and he begs God to keep him from sin, knowing that his prayers would not be accepted unless he guarded against sin. We must be as sincere for God's grace in us as we are for his favor toward us.

He prays that he will not say any sinful words: *"Set a guard, O LORD, over my mouth; keep watch over the door of my lips!"* (v. 3). Good people know the evil of tongue-sins, and how easily we say them (when enemies provoke us, we are in danger of carrying our resentment too far, and speaking out-of-turn, as Moses did). We must keep our mouths as a bridle keeps a horse's, but even that will not be enough. We must pray to God to keep them. Nehemiah prayed to the Lord when he set a watch, and so must we because without him the watchman patrols in vain.

That he might not lean toward any sinful ways: *"Do not let my heart incline to any evil to busy myself with wicked deeds"* (v. 4). The people around us, and the pressure of those against us, can stir up and bring out our corrupt instincts. We are ready to do what others do and to think that if we have been hurt we can retaliate. Therefore, we need to pray that we will never be left to ourselves to behave sinfully, either with or against others. While we live in such an evil world and have such evil hearts, we need to pray that we will not be drawn in by any temptation or pressured to commit sin.

That he might not be caught up in sinful pleasures: *"Let me not eat of their delicacies!"* (v. 4). It is better to eat vegetables or herbs, away from temptation, than get fat on the meat of sin. Sinners pretend to find wonderful things in sin—stolen waters are sweet; forbidden fruit is pleasing to look at. But when we think about how soon the delicacies of sin will turn into something bitter, which it eventually will (like the bite or sting of a snake), we will be afraid of those delicacies. Then we will pray to God to remove them from our sight, and by his grace to turn us against them. Good people will even pray against the sweets of sin.

Daily Reflection

Many of the psalms are either very honest prayers or incredible songs of praise to God. Either way, they are very real and provide us with a candid look into someone else's prayer life. David was someone who prayed and sang a lot, the psalms are a testimony to his heart before God. Reading through them, we can identify with certain ones depending on our circumstances or season in life. When it comes to our favorites, psalm 141 may not be one of the most visited ones, but it is just as revealing in its sincerity. Here, we only see the first few lines, and already it shows us so much about real prayer.

1. Henry says that David "begs God to hear and answer his prayers." Do you think he is correct in saying this?
2. Do you ever ask God to listen to you when you begin praying, or do you just start with your needs and wants?
3. Why is incense often used as an analogy for prayer in the Bible? Read Revelation 8:4.
4. Why do you think David's next section of prayer turns to God keeping and delivering him?

26

SOLOMON'S PRAYER

O LORD God, do not turn away the face of your anointed one!
Remember your steadfast love for David your servant
2 Chronicles 6:42

Solomon brings appropriate requests in his prayer in 2 Chronicles 6:

That God would own this house, and see it as the place where he said he would put his name (v. 20). He could not have asked God to show such favor to this house above any other if he had not said that it should be his rest forever. A quickly-answered prayer must be guaranteed by the word. We can pray to God in humble confidence to be pleased with us in Jesus because he said he was pleased in him—*"This is my beloved Son"* (Matt. 3:17).

That God would hear and accept the prayers from or about that place (v. 21). He did not ask God to help them whether they prayed for themselves or not, but that God would help them in answer to their prayers. Even Jesus' intercessions do not supersede but encourage our requests. He prayed that God would hear from heaven. He lives in heaven, not his temple, so help must come from there. "When you hear, forgive." The forgiveness of our sins makes way for all the other answers to our prayers.

That God would judge all requests fairly (v. 23). We can pray for this because we are sure it will be done. God is on the throne judging fairly.

That God would have mercy on his people when they repented, turned, and looked for him (v. 24-31, 36-39). This we can pray for, building on God's repeated declarations that he is ready to accept repentant people.

That God would allow strangers into this house, and answer their prayers (v. 32-33).

That God would always own and plead the cause of his people and not those who oppose them (v. 34). That he would uphold their cause (v. 35). If they are the Israel of God, their cause is the cause of God, and he will support it.

He concludes this prayer with some expressions he learned from his father, borrowed from Psalm 132:8-10. The whole word of God can be used to direct us in prayer—how can we express ourselves better to God than in the language of his own Spirit? These words directed Solomon because they had reference to the work he was doing. He prays:

That God would own the temple, and make it his resting place: *"You and the ark"* (v. 41). What good is the ark without the God of the ark?

That he would bless the ministers of the temple: *"Clothed with salvation"* (v. 41)—do not just save them, but let them save others by offering the sacrifices of righteousness.

That the service of the temple will be for the joy and satisfaction of all the Lord's people: *"Let your saints rejoice in your goodness"* (v. 41). *"We shall be satisfied with the goodness of your house, the holiness of your temple!"* (Psalm 65:4).

In the last sentence, he pleads two things:

His own relation to God: *"O LORD God, do not turn away the face of your anointed one!"* (v. 42)

God's covenant with his father: *"Remember your steadfast love for David your servant"* (v. 42).

We can plead with God in the same way Solomon does here: "We deserve that God should turn away our face, that he should reject us and our prayers, but we come in the name of Jesus, your chosen Messiah, your Christ. You always hear him, and he will never turn away his face. We have no righteousness of our own to plead, but Lord, remember the mercies of David your servant." Jesus is God's servant (Isa. 42:1), and is called David, (Hos. 3:5). "Lord, remember his mercies, and accept us on the account of them. Remember his concern for his Father's honor and man's salvation, and how he suffered because of that. Remember the promises of the everlasting covenant, which grace has brought us in Jesus —the mercies of David" (Isa. 55:3, Acts 13:34). This must be our desire and hope, our prayer and plea, because all of it is our salvation.

Daily Reflection

Working through these reflections, you may find it helpful to share some of your personal insights with others. We can always get a healthy view of things when we hear the opinions of people around us. Sometimes, they may even shed some truth where we are blind to it. Open up to someone you trust, not just anybody (especially if it's very personal!). If you are looking for more understanding on a topic, consult someone you know who is grounded in faith and knowledge. We are not meant to figure out everything on our own, and you may find it enriching to learn along with others in a group.

1. Do you notice any similarities between Solomon's Prayer and the Lord's Prayer?
2. There is a huge focus on the temple in this prayer, obviously because Solomon built it. Do you ever pray in a similar fashion for your church?
3. Do you ever pray for your leaders, ministers, pastors, and others who serve the church?
4. It seems odd that God should be reminded, but Solomon asks that he "remember" his love. What does this mean?

27

PAUL'S THANKSGIVING PRAYER

We give thanks to God always for all of you,
constantly mentioning you in our prayers
1 Thessalonians 1:2

Paul begins with thanksgiving to God, who is the author of everything good that comes to us, or is done by us. God is the object of our prayer and praise. Even when we do not actually give thanks to God through our words, we should have a grateful sense of God's goodness. Paul did not only give thanks to those who were his closest friends, or most favored of God, but for all of them.

He linked prayer with thanksgiving. When we make our requests known to God, we should join thanksgiving to it (Phil. 4:6). We should pray always and without ceasing, and should not only pray for ourselves, but for others also. Since there are lots to be thankful for ourselves and our friends, there are many reasons for the constant prayer for all our needs.

He mentions the specifics for which he was so thankful to God:

Their faith and their work of faith. Their *"faith in God has gone forth everywhere"* (1 Thess. 1:8). Their faith was a true and living faith because it was a working faith. Wherever there is true faith, it will work—it will have an influence on the heart and life, and it will encourage us to work for God and our own salvation. We are encouraged in our own faith and the faith of others when we see the work of faith. *"I will show you my faith by my works"* (Jam. 2:18).

Their love and labor of love. Love will remain and be perfected in the life to come. Faith works by love, it shows itself in our love for God and love for our neighbor.

Their hope and the patience of hope. We are saved by hope. This grace is compared to the soldier's helmet and sailor's anchor and is useful in times of danger. Wherever there is a solid hope of eternal life, it will appear by the exercise of patience—in patient endurance in hardships and patient waiting for the glory to come. *"If we hope for what we do not see, we wait for it with patience"* (Rom. 8:25).

Paul sees that faith, hope, and love come from Jesus. He mentions the fountain these virtues flow from—God's love that has chosen us: *"For we know, brothers loved by God, that he has chosen you"* (1 Thess. 1:4). Speaking of their election, he calls them brothers, because the brotherhood between Christians is election. And it is a good reason why we should love one another, because we are all loved by God, and were loved by him when there was nothing in us to deserve his love.

All those who are called and sanctified were chosen for salvation before eternity.

The election of God is of his own good pleasure and grace, not because any of those who are chosen deserve it.

The election of God may be known by the fruits that are shown as a result.

Whenever we are giving thanks to God for his grace for ourselves or others, we should run up the streams to the fountain and give thanks to God for his love that has chosen us.

Another reason for Paul's thanksgiving is the success of his ministry among them. He was thankful on his own account as well as theirs, that he had not worked for nothing. Their ready acceptance of the gospel he preached to them was evidence of their being chosen and loved by God. He acknowledges that the gospel did not only come to them in word but in power. They did not only hear it but submitted to the power of it. It did not just tickle the ear or fill their heads with ideas and amuse their minds for a while, but it affected their hearts—a spiritual power convinced their consciences and changed their lives. This is how we know we are chosen if we do not only speak of the things of God like parrots, but feel the influence of them in our hearts, killing our lusts, bringing us out from the world, and raising us up to heavenly things.

The gospel came by the Holy Spirit. Wherever the gospel comes in power, it is to be attributed to the work of the Holy Spirit. Unless the Spirit of God accompanies the word of God, to give it power, it will be dead words. *"The letter kills, but the Spirit gives life"* (2 Cor. 3:6). The gospel also came to them in confidence. They were completely convinced of the truth of it, not easily shaken in their minds by objections and doubts. They were willing to leave everything for Jesus. The word was not like the sentiments of some philosophers about opinions and speculations, but the object of their faith and assurance. Their faith was the evidence of things not seen.

Daily Reflection

Many of Paul's letters begin with a greeting and also his admitting that he prays for his fellow Christians in the different churches and regions. It was very important for him to keep all the brothers and sisters in prayer because he realized it was not his message or any of the apostles that kept the people close to God. In the end, it was God who kept each one by his Spirit. He not only prayed for them but thanked God for answering his prayers concerning them

1. If you had to give a percentage to how much of your prayers are requests and how much are thanks, what would the result look like?

2. Do you only thank God for the prayers he has answered, or is there more you are grateful for?
3. Why is it important to thank God for other Christians and their spiritual growth?
4. Read Colossians 4:2, Philippians 4:6, 1 Thessalonians 5:18, and Ephesians 5:20.
5. What does it mean to be elected or chosen by God? Why is it so important to be grateful for this?

28

NEHEMIAH'S PRAYER

Let your ear be attentive and your eyes open,
to hear the prayer of your servant that I now pray before you.
Nehemiah 1:6

Nehemiah's prayer refers to all the prayers he had sent to God day and night, while he was mourning the destruction of Jerusalem, and the request he was bringing to the king for his favor to Jerusalem. We can see the following in this prayer:

His humble and reverent address to God—he goes low before him and gives the glory due to his name (v. 5). It is the same approach as Daniel's (Dan. 9:4). It teaches us that we must draw near to God:

with a holy awe of his majesty and glory, remembering that he is the God of heaven, sovereign Lord over us, infinitely above all principalities and powers, angels, and kings. He is a

God to be worshiped with fear by all his people, and whose judgment his enemies should be afraid of.

with a holy confidence in his grace and truth, because he keeps his covenant and mercy for those that love him, not only what is promised, but more.

His general request for the audience and acceptance of all the prayers and confessions he made to God. *"Let your ear be attentive and your eyes open, to hear the prayer of your servant that I now pray before you"* (v. 6). God created the eyes and ears, and so will he not see clearly or hear attentively?

His penitent confession of sin. It was not only Israel who had sinned, but *"I and my father's house have sinned"* (v. 6). He humbles himself in this confession. *"We have acted very corruptly against you"* (v. 7). In the confession of sin, let these two things be owned—the corruption of ourselves in opposition to the commands of God and the offense it is to God.

The pleas he urges for mercy for his people Israel.

He reminds God what he said about them, the rule in his proceedings toward them, which might be the rule of their expectations from him (v. 8-9). He had said that if they broke the covenant with him, he would scatter them among the nations, and that was fulfilled in their captivity. But, he also said that if they turned to him (as they began to do, renouncing idolatry and keeping temple service), he would gather them again. He quotes this from Deuteronomy 30:1-5 and begs God to remember it (even though the Eternal Mind does not need reminding). Lord, remember the word which you commanded to your servant Moses. Our best pleas in prayer are those that are taken from the promise of God, the word on which he has caused us to hope (Psalm 119:49).

He pleads the relation between them and God: *"They are your servants and your people, whom you have redeemed by your great power and by your strong hand"* (v. 10). "Will you allow your enemies to trample on and oppress your servants? If you will not appear for your people, who will you appear for?" As evidence of their being God's servants, he gives them this character—*"your servants"* (v. 11). "They fear your name, they are not only called by your name but have a reverence for your name. They now worship you, and you only, according to your will, this is what they desire to do."

He pleads the great things God had already done for them. *"Whom you have redeemed by your great power and by your strong hand"* (v. 10). "Your power is still the same, will you not redeem them and perfect their redemption? Do not let those who have a powerful God on their side be overpowered."

Lastly, he concludes with a specific petition, that God would prosper him in what he did, and give him favor with the king. He calls him a *"man"* (v. 11) because the greatest of men are just men before God. *"Who are you that you are afraid of man?"* (Isa. 51:12). Mercy from this man is what he prays for, meaning not the king's mercy, but mercy from God in his address to the king. Favor with men is then encouraging when we can see it comes from the mercy of God.

Daily Reflection

Here we have another example of a prayer from the Bible. By looking at these men that were greatly used by God and the way they prayed, we can model ourselves on the attitudes they had before God and the methods they used that were so effective. Nehemiah may not be listed among the major prophets or kings, but through his leadership, he brought the people back to Jerusalem to rebuild the walls. His integrity as a follower of God and the way he interceded for his people is an example enough for us to look at.

1. Is it possible to come to God humbly and confidently at the same time? See Hebrews 4:6.
2. Do you ever ask God to listen to you, or do you just assume he already is?
3. Why does Nehemiah add in a confession when he is asking God for something?
4. A plea is similar to using an argument in our prayer to God. What are the different pleas Nehemiah brings?
5. Why do we also sometimes need to pray for favor with people?

29

HANNAH'S THANKSGIVING

"My heart exults in the LORD;
my horn is exalted in the LORD.
My mouth derides my enemies,
because I rejoice in your salvation."
1 Samuel 2:1

Here is Hannah's thanksgiving—not only a prayer but also a prophecy. Here, she gives back praise out of the fullness of a deeply affected heart, her mouth spoke.

When she had received mercy from God she received it with thankfulness, praising God. Not like the nine lepers in Luke 17:17. Praise is our rent, our tribute. We are unjust if we do not pay it.

The mercy she had received was an answer to prayer, and so she felt obliged to give thanks for it. What we win by prayer we may wear with comfort and must wear with praise.

Her thanksgiving is called a prayer. Hannah prayed because thanksgiving is an important part of prayer. In every address to God, we must be grateful to him as our benefactor. Thanksgiving for blessings received is accepted as a request for more blessings.

Her prayer was in her mind. Her voice was not heard, but in her thanksgiving, she spoke so that everyone might hear her. She made her supplication with groanings that could not be spoken, but her lips were opened to reveal God's praise.

This thanksgiving is here written in the Bible for the encouragement of everyone to attend the throne of grace. God will regard our prayers and praises.

In this prayer, we can see Hannah's victory in God, his glorious attributes, and the great things he had done for her.

What great things she says of God. She takes little notice of the specific mercy she was rejoicing about and does not speak of Samuel as the prettiest child, the most sensible child that she ever saw, as parents often do. She overlooks the gift, and praises the giver, whereas most people forget the giver and focus only on the gift. Every stream should lead us to the fountain, and the blessings we receive from God should turn our admiration to the attributes of God. There may be other Samuels, but no other Jehovah. *"There is none holy like the LORD"* (v. 2). God is to be praised as having no rival and of unparalleled perfection. This glory is due to his name, to show there is none like him, and none beside him. All others were pretenders (Psalm 18:31). Hannah celebrates four of God's glorious attributes:

His perfect purity. This is an attribute most praised in heaven by those that always see his face (Isa. 6:3, Rev. 4:8). So, in Hannah's triumph, *"There is none holy like the LORD"* (v. 2). It is the righteousness of his nature, his infinite agreement with himself, and the justice of his government and judgment. When we remember this, we should give thanks.

His almighty power. There is no rock (or any strength) like our God. Hannah experienced incredible support by holding onto him, and so she speaks about what she found and seems to refer to that of Moses (Deut. 32:31).

His unsearchable wisdom. The Lord, the Judge of all, is a God of knowledge. He clearly and perfectly sees into the character of every person and the merits of every cause, and he gives knowledge and understanding to those that seek them of him.

His unerring justice. By him, actions are weighed. He is just in his eternal counsel. The actions of the children of men are held accountable, in the balances of his judgment, so that he will repay every person according to their work, and is not mistaken about what any person is or does.

How she encourages herself in these things. What we give God the glory for we can be encouraged in. Hannah does so in the following:

In holy joy. *"My heart exults in the LORD."* Not so much in her son as in her God. He is the gladness of our joy (Psalm 43:4), and our joy must not be found in anything short of him.

In holy triumph. *"My horn is exalted in the LORD."* Her reputation was not just saved by having a son but lifted up by having a son. My horn is exalted means "My praises are elevated." Exalted in the Lord—God is to have the honor of all our exaltations, and in him we have victory.

Then Hannah silences those that set up themselves as enemies of God. *"Talk no more so very proudly"* (v. 3). Do not let Peninnah and her children rebuke her anymore because of her confidence in God and praying to him. In the end, she found it was not for nothing. *"Then my enemy will see, and shame will cover her who said to me, 'Where is the LORD your God?'"* (Micah 7:10). Or perhaps it was beneath her to notice Peninnah and her malice in this song. This is intended to stop the insolence of the Philistines, and other enemies of God and Israel, that set their mouths against the heavens (Psalm 73:9). *"Let not arrogance come from your mouth"* (v. 3).

Daily Reflection

Hannah was Samuel's mother. She had prayed and waited for so long for a child before God finally gave her what she wanted. But instead of just accepting the reply and the gift, Hannah's thanks are recorded in the Bible as an example and a testimony of what a true, grateful prayer should look like. The words might seem a bit outdated or over-the-top in our modern language, but the heart of what she says is what we are most concerned with. Her attitude of thanks is what makes this prayer shine.

1. Do you thank God for giving you the things you have asked for, or do you thank him for the mercy and grace he gives without being asked to do so?

2. What do the words exult and exalt mean? You may have to look them up.
3. Why do you think Hannah mentions her enemies while she is giving thanks?
4. Do you ever thank God for his purity, power, wisdom, or justice?
5. If you had to write a thanksgiving prayer to the Lord, what would it sound like?

30

JESUS PRAYS FOR THE DISCIPLES TO BE KEPT

"Holy Father, keep them in your name, which you have given me."
John 17:11

The first thing Jesus prays for is to commit them to his Father's care. Their danger came from the world, and he asks that they might be kept from this evil. The request itself is *"Keep them from the evil one."* He does not pray that they would be taken out of the world.

The easiest way to protect them would be to remove them to a better world. But Jesus does not pray this for his disciples, because he came to conquer those emotions which make people impatient of life, and stubborn for death. It is his will that we should take up our cross, not leave it behind. Though Jesus loves his disciples, he does not call them to heaven, but leaves them for some time in this world, so that they may do good and glorify God on earth, and be made ready for heaven. Many good people are spared to live because they cannot be spared to die. It is more of an honor for a Christian soldier to overcome the world by faith than to retreat from it by a monastic vow, and more an honor to serve Jesus in a city than to serve him in a closed-up room.

Another way is by keeping them from the corruption that is in the world. He prays they will be kept in this way (v. 11, 15). There are four parts to Jesus' request:

"Holy Father." The title of the one he prays to is important. He speaks to God as a holy Father. In committing ourselves and others to godly care, we can be encouraged by his holiness, because this is engaged for the protection of his holy people. *"I have sworn by my holiness"* (Psalm 89:35). If he is a holy God and hates sin, he will make us holy, and keep us from sin. If he is a Father, he will take care of his children, he will teach them, and keep them.

"Keep them." Keep them from evil, or out of evil. He had taught them to pray every day, *"Deliver us from evil"* (Matt. 6:13), and this would encourage them to pray.

Keep them from the evil one, the devil and all his schemes—that wicked one and all his followers. Keep them from Satan as a tempter, that he may not be able to sift them, or that their faith may not fail. Keep them from him as a destroyer, that he may not drive them to despair.

Keep them from the evil thing, that is sin—from everything that looks like it, or leads to it. Keep them, that they would do nothing evil (2 Cor. 13:7). Sin is evil which we should hate and fear.

Keep them from the evil of the world, and of their trials in it, so that it may not harm them—not that they will be kept from hardship, but kept through it.

"In your name."

Keep them for your name's sake. Your name and honor are involved in their preservation as well as mine because both will suffer if they either turn away or fail. The Old Testament saints often pleaded, "for thy name's sake." We can also plead this way knowing that we are more concerned about the honor of God's name than our own.

Keep them in your name. "Keep them in the knowledge and fear of your name. Keep them in the service of your name, whatever it costs them. Keep them in the interest of your name, and let them always be faithful to this. Keep them in your truths, in your commandments.

Keep them by or through your name. Keep them by your power, in your hand. Keep them yourself, undertake for them, and let them be your own immediate care. Keep them by whatever protection you yourself have appointed, and by which you have made yourself known. Keep them by your word and commands. Let your name be their strong tower, your temple their covering.

"Which you have given me." He speaks of the disciples as those whom the Father had given him. What we receive as our Father's gifts, we may comfortably give back into our Father's care. "Father, keep the virtues, qualities, and comforts you have given me, the children you have given me, and the ministry I have received."

Daily Reflection

John 17 is one of the most incredible passages in the Bible because we get a glimpse into Jesus' prayers. There is no doubt he prayed every day and prayed often, but not many of those words are recorded, probably because they were personal and private. But here, he prays a very special prayer in the company of his disciples. It is a prayer for them. We have an amazing example of how we should pray for ourselves and others. We are also shown what is important enough for Jesus to ask his Father for.

1. Why doesn't God just take us out of the world rather than leave us here?
2. In the context of this prayer, what does it mean for God to keep us?
3. Why was Jesus praying for his disciples?
4. Why is it important to pray in the Father's name or in Jesus' name? Read John 14:13.
5. Do you ever pray that others will be kept safe from evil, safe from harm?

31

JESUS PRAYS FOR UNITY

"I do not ask for these only, *but also for those who will believe in me through their word,*
that they may all be one, just as you, Father, are in me, and I in you,
that they also may be in us,
so that the world may believe that you have sent me."
John 17:20-21

Who is included in this prayer? *"I do not ask for these only, but also for those who will believe in me through their word"* (v. 20). Those who are interested in the reconciliation of Jesus, that do, or will, believe in him. This is who is described, and it shows the character and duty of a Christian.

What is meant in this prayer? *"That they may all be one."* (v. 21). The same was said before in verse 11, and again in verse 22. This was the heart of Jesus. This unity is not just for the disciples as ministers and apostles, that they might be one in their testimony to Jesus, but it is for all believers. It is the prayer of Jesus for everyone that is his, and we can be sure it is an answered prayer—*"That they may all be one"* (v. 21), *"one even as we are one"* (v. 22), *"may become perfectly one"* (v. 23). We see three things in this unity:

That we might all be incorporated into one body. As Jesus died, so he prayed, to gather us all in one (John 11:52, Eph. 1:10).

That we might all be inspired by one Spirit. Union with the Father and Son is obtained and kept only by the Holy Spirit. We are joined to the Lord in one spirit (1 Cor. 6:17).

That we might all be united in the bond of love—all of one heart. That we all may be one, not in every little thing—this is neither possible nor necessary, but in the great things of God.

What is his request? Unity. Jesus' plan was to bring mankind to God. *"And might reconcile us both to God in one body"* (Eph. 2:15-16). This speaks about uniting Jews and Gentiles in the church—that great mystery, that the Gentiles should be joint-heirs, and of the same body (Eph. 3:6). This is what Jesus' prayer refers to, it is the one thing he aimed at in dying. Those words, *"I in them and you in me"* (v. 23), show what that union is. First, Union with Christ: *"I in them."* Jesus living in the hearts of believers is the life and soul of the new person. Secondly, Union with God through him: *"You in me,"* to be in them. Thirdly, Union with each other, resulting from these: *"that they may become perfectly one."* We are complete in him.

He prays that the disciples be given his glory. *"The glory that you have given me I have given to them, that they may be one even as we are one"* (v. 22). He gave it to them, that they might be one. First, to entitle them to the privilege of unity, that through their relation to the Father and Jesus, they would be one. The gift of the Spirit, that great glory which the Father gave to the Son, is given to all believers, and makes us one because he works all in all (1 Cor. 12:4). Secondly, to engage them in the duty of unity. That in agreeing and communion in one creed and one covenant, one Spirit and one Bible—in what they have in one God and one Christ, and of what they hope for in one heaven, they may be of one mind and one mouth. Worldly glory puts people against each other because if some are ahead, others are behind. So, while the disciples dreamed of a physical kingdom, they were always quarreling. But spiritual honors are given to all believers, there is no place for competition. The more Christians are concerned with the glory Jesus has given them, the less they will want their own glory, and be less likely to quarrel.

He pleads for the influence their unity would have on others. This is said twice: *"So that the world may believe that you have sent me"* (v. 21), and, *"So that the world may know that you sent me and loved them even as you loved me"* (v. 23). He wants all people to be saved, and to come to the knowledge of the truth (1 Tim. 2:4, 2 Pet. 3:9). Therefore, it is his will that all means possible should be used for the conviction and conversion of the world. We do not know who is chosen, but we must in our places do our best to preach salvation, and watch that we do nothing to stop it. The fruit of the church's unity will be evidence of the truth of Christianity and a way of bringing many people to embrace it.

Daily Reflection

Unity is a very precious thing that the world often tries to manufacture or conjure up, but there cannot be true unity unless it is in the Spirit! Jesus understood this when he prayed for his disciples. He knew that the Father would have to intervene if there was any chance of these men drawing closer together in a spiritual sense. Despite their different backgrounds, opinions, and personalities, God could unite them in a common faith. We need to look carefully at this because if there is no unity among us in the church, it will not last.

1. Who was Jesus praying for in this prayer?
2. Why is unity such an important aspect of God?
3. Do you ever pray for unity in your own church amongst your fellow Christians?
4. Why is unity in the church so important for the rest of the world to see?
5. Read 1 Corinthians 1:10. What does this say about unity?

IF YOU ENJOYED this devotional book on prayer and you are eager to learn more about this effective tool for communicating with God and maturing your relationship with Jesus, why not find these other titles? They are all written by classic Christian writers explaining prayer using the Bible.

- E.M. Bounds Prayer: *31 Life-Changing Insights from E.M. Bounds on How to Pray with Daily Reflections*
- J.C. Ryle on Prayer: *31 Insights for Understanding the Purpose and Power of Prayer*
- C.H. Spurgeon on Prayer: *31 Effective Insights on How to Pray with Daily Reflections*
- John Bunyan on Prayer: *31 Biblical Insights for Effective Prayer*
- George Muller on Prayer: *31 Prayer Insights for Developing an Intimate Relationship with God*

ABOUT MATTHEW HENRY

Matthew Henry was born into a Christian family in 1662. He was raised in the teachings of the Bible, with morning and evening family devotions. It is believed Henry could read the Bible at the age of three! His father, Phillip, was a minister but had been kicked out of the church for refusing to use the new forms of liturgy introduced by the Act of Uniformity.

Growing up under his father's scriptural teaching, Henry was struck by the verse in Psalm 51 that says, *"A broken and contrite heart, O God, you will not despise."* This would later lead him to salvation and giving his life to the Lord. At the age of ten, he became seriously ill with a fever and was convicted of his sin and about hell after listening to a sermon.

He was not allowed to attend Oxford or Cambridge because of his father's non-conformism, so he went to an academy under a man called Thomas Doolittle before returning to learn at home when it was closed down. After a while, he went back to London but was not happy studying law and left the college after less than a year. It was at this time, while he was back at home, that he was asked by a friend to preach, and as a result of his passion and well-prepared sermons, he began to receive invitations to share at other meetings.

In 1687, he was ordained as a minister and agreed to pastor a congregation in Chester. He would remain in that position for 25 years, overseeing the church. From a handful of members in the beginning, he eventually had to extend the building to house the increasing number of his congregants.

Henry was married in 1689, but after his wife died in childbirth, he remarried a few years later to a woman named Mary. There were also complications when it came to having children, with three of their children dying shortly after being born. But Henry kept his eyes on God rather than blaming him, saying, "The Lord is righteous, He takes and gives, and gives and takes again."

Despite all this, he still found time to begin work in 1704 on what would become his famous *Commentary on the Whole Bible*. At the time of his death, he had completed Genesis to Acts. (The remainder of the work up until the end of Revelation was put together by a group of friends using his copious notes.) Having learned Latin and Greek as a child, he had an obvious advantage in understanding the original texts, helping him in his theological insights of the Bible.

His attentive research and diligent preparation of his sermons and written work are evident in his preaching and books. Most of the time he was behind a pulpit bringing a word to a congregation, Henry would use an expository speaking style—basing his sermon on one or two verses and expanding on them. His approach was to "choose for your pulpit subjects the plainest, and most needful truths, and endeavor to make them plainer." He would do his best to stick as closely to the literal interpretation of verses as possible, and this is what made his work simple yet profound.

He gained popularity as a preacher and teacher of the Bible as his *Commentary* began to be published. This resulted in him being invited to share in many meetings and eventually accepting a post to be minister at a Chapel at Hackney in London in 1712. A few years before this, however, his health had begun to show signs of the stress of preaching so much, and he fainted or struggled with fever.

But this never stopped him from traveling to different churches to preach, especially his very first congregation in Chester. It was on a trip to this area in 1714 when he was thrown off his horse, but instead of admitting he was badly injured, Henry continued to the next church, where he shared the gospel despite not feeling well. After this, he could not travel any further and spent the night at a house where he died from complications.

Matthew Henry left an indelible mark on Christian literature in the form of his *Commentary,* with George Whitefield, Charles Spurgeon, and John Wesley admitting to its assistance in their ministries. It has continued to be one of the most read books alongside the Bible for those studying for deeper scriptural understanding. It is no surprise that Henry's work helped to shape the spirituality and Christian convictions of many in the centuries after his death.

BIBLIOGRAPHY

Crossway. (2001). *English Standard Version Bible*. Crossway Bibles.
Henry, M. (2009). *Matthew Henry's commentary on the whole Bible*. Hendrickson Publishers.
Henry, M. (2016). *A method for prayer*. Lulu.com.
Thomas Nelson Publishers. (2014). *Holy Bible, KJV*. Thomas Nelson Pub.

www.ingramcontent.com/pod-product-compliance
Lightning Source LLC
LaVergne TN
LVHW010220070526
838199LV00062B/4671